MACARON MAGIC

MACARON MAGIC

Jialin Tian, Ph.D.

Photographs and Design by Jialin Tian
Step-by-Step Photographs by Yabin Yu

Macaron Magic

Jialin Tian, Ph.D.

Published in the United States by
Jayca Inc.
P. O. Box 2451
Poquoson, VA 23662
USA

Photographs and styling: Jialin Tian
Step-by-step photographs and author's photographs: Yabin Yu
Book design and layout: Jialin Tian
Production manager: Yabin Yu

www.macaronmagic.com

ISBN 978-0-9837764-0-6

First Edition

To my mother, Yabin

CONTENTS

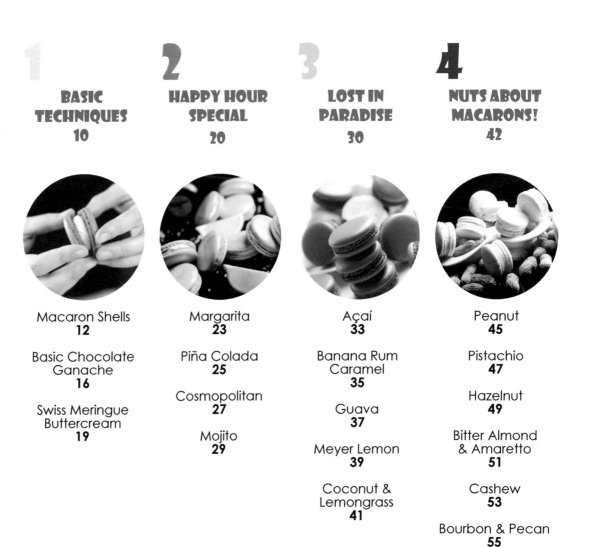

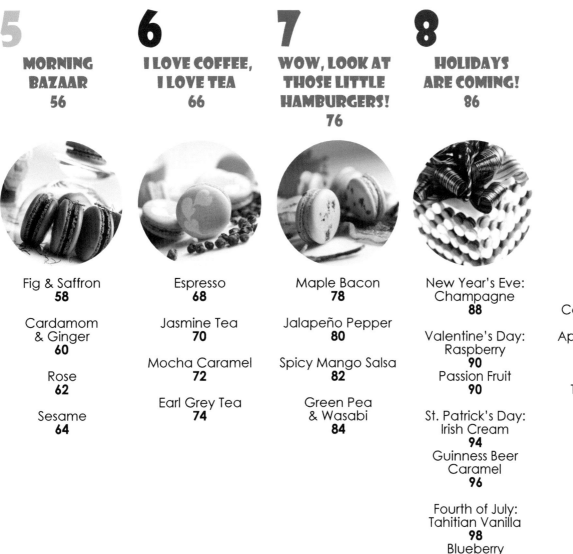

INTRODUCTION

Almonds, sugar, egg whites, and magic! Although its origin is debatable, we can all agree that the Parisian macaron we know today is a symphony of sweet delight with endless possibilities. At first glance, you see a round sandwich-like miniature pastry with a glossy, smooth, and colorful exterior. A closer inspection shows that the macaron's shiny thin shells are supported by airy, spongy "feet" underneath, which make the macaron look like a pair of disproportional button mushrooms. The two shells are held together by a mysterious interior soon to be discovered. Now you have seen enough, let's take a bite! The outer crust is slightly crisp but delicate, beneath the crust is moist and tender, the final crescendo ends on the velvety, smooth, and decadent center. The macaron is gone before you even realize it! Now you are eager to try another one, but who can blame you? No one can resist these rainbow-colored little gems filled with an array of sinfully delicious fillings.

I always imagined that Parisian macarons were discovered by accident. Imagine that in a dark and cramped kitchen an exhausted young apprentice works on the last batch of traditional macarons. His arms become robotic from performing the same repetitive movements. He folds the meringue into the almond paste when he is half conscious and half asleep. Before he knows it, it's too late! The meringue was overworked and has collapsed. By now, he is fully awake and starts to become anxious; there is no time to make another batch! He is terrified by the imminent scrutiny of his master, but what can he do? Panicked, he quickly pipes out the macarons, loads them into the oven, and prays for the best. Imagine the relief he feels when the accident turns out to be an unexpected success. Like many "accidental" discoveries, it may take a remarkable event to stumble on success, but it takes an even more remarkable talent to recreate and perfect that success.

Making the perfect macaron is no accident since many factors can affect the outcome of the final product. Variables such as the texture of the almond flour, the temperature and state of the sugar, the moisture content of the egg whites, and the viscosity of the macaron batter as well as random environmental variables such as ambient temperature and humidity can all play a crucial role in macaron baking. Fortunately, these factors can be controlled so that we can achieve a consistent result regardless of minor changes in baking conditions. Nevertheless, some trial-and-error experimentation may still be required.

I discovered the joy of pastry experimentation when I was a graduate student. At the time, I was working on my doctoral dissertation on the reconstruction of irregularly sampled interferograms for an imaging Fourier transform spectrometer, an optical instrument for remote-sensing satellite applications. Two years into my research, I became increasingly frustrated with not having found a solution. I started to question whether a solution even existed. That was when I began to bake. Making pastries helped me to see the problem from a fresh new angle. Sometimes, even when my baking experiment was disastrous, the process made me realize that a failed attempt brings me another step closer to success, assuming a finite number of solutions exist.

With the guidance of this book, I encourage you to try your hand at making these delectable treats at home, and don't feel frustrated even if they don't turn out the way you have envisioned on the first try. The book is divided into eight chapters. In the first chapter, we introduce the fundamental technique for making the perfect macaron shells. We discuss in detail how to control the three key factors—temperature, moisture, and viscosity—to produce the perfect result every time. We present the concept of "quasi-meringue" in the most crucial step of macaron making. In the next six chapters, we explore some of the endless possibilities for making the most delicious macarons, from your favorite happy hour special to an exotic tropical paradise, from the land of coffee and tea to the morning bazaar, from an array of nutty transformations to a sweet-and-savory wonderland. In the final chapter, we celebrate the most memorable days of the year with macarons! From timeless classics to innovative creations to spectacular showpieces, these little wonders will definitely make a lasting impression. Finally, we have included a list of resources for the tools and ingredients used in this book.

The "macaron project" would never have become a reality without the help of my mother, Yabin. From taking the step-by-step photographs to shopping for ingredients, from critiquing my photographs to helping out with the dishes, she has done it all! If I am a piano virtuoso, then she must be my backup orchestra; together we performed a concerto of irresistible wonders. An orchestra cannot perform without a stage manager, and that honor goes to my father Richard. I thank him for all the assistance he has provided during the making of this book; in addition, I want to thank him for always being on standby to offer a helping hand. My deepest appreciation goes to the chefs and instructors who have shared their invaluable knowledge and experience with me. My special thanks go to Chef Stéphane Glacier for teaching me the art of making the perfect macaron. Finally, many thanks to my "tasters and testers"; it's a tough job, but someone has to do it!

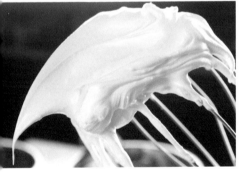

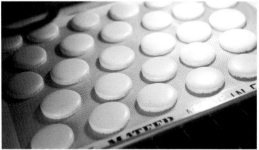

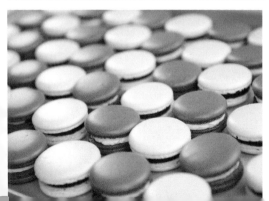

BASIC TECHNIQUES

In this chapter, we introduce the fundamental techniques for making the perfect macaron shell. In addition, we provide recipes for basic chocolate ganache and Swiss meringue buttercream fillings. These recipes serve as the basis for the rest of the book.

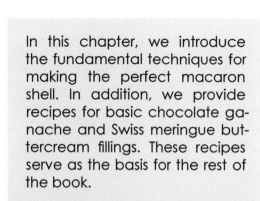

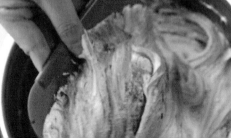

MACARON SHELLS

In this foundational recipe, we introduce the technique for making the perfect macaron shell. We discuss the importance of three key factors that can determine the success of the final product: temperature, moisture, and viscosity. We explore methods for precisely controlling these factors and how to use them to our advantage. In addition, we introduce the concept of "quasi-meringue" in the most crucial step of macaron making.

Yield: Shells for about 85 to 90 1½-in/3.8-cm filled macarons

INGREDIENTS

4 oz/113 g aged egg whites (about 4 egg whites), at room temperature

2 cups (10.58 oz/300 g) blanched whole almonds or 2⅔ cups (10.58 oz/300 g) blanched almond flour

1½ cups (10.58 oz/300 g) granulated sugar

Powdered food coloring, water soluble (optional)

Italian Meringue:

4 oz/113 g fresh egg whites (about 4 egg whites), at room temperature

½ tsp (0.035 oz/1 g) dried egg white powder

1½ cups (10.58 oz/300 g) granulated sugar

⅓ cup (2.67 fl oz/79 ml) distilled water

Note: In this recipe, we introduce three means to improve the stability of the macaron batter. By using aged egg whites in the almond-sugar paste and dried egg whites in the meringue, we can control the moisture content with a higher degree of precision. In addition, by using Italian meringue, we can further enhance the stability. The resulting macaron batter is less sensitive to environmental variations such as ambient temperature and humidity.

1. On the day before baking, separate four eggs and place the egg whites in a mixing bowl. Loosely cover the bowl with plastic wrap and refrigerate overnight. Reserve the yolks for another use.

2. One hour before baking, take the aged egg whites out of the refrigerator and allow them to return to room temperature.

3. Meanwhile, combine blanched whole almonds and sugar **(1)**. Process the almond-sugar mixture in a food processor for about 15 seconds or until the mixture becomes a fine powder **(2, 3)**. Do not over-mix. Pour the mixture into a medium-sized mixing bowl and reserve.

Note: If you use store-bought almond flour, make sure it is fresh by checking the expiration date. Combine the almond flour and sugar in a food processor bowl, and pulse the machine a few times. There are several benefits to using a food processor to process the almond flour and sugar. First, a food processor can combine the ingredients thoroughly; second, it can eliminate the lumps in the almond flour and give the flour a finer texture; and third, it can pulverize the granulated sugar into powdered sugar. (Avoid using store-bought powdered sugar since it may contain cornstarch, used to prevent clumping.)

Note: The viscosity of the batter is crucial to the success of the final product. If the batter is under-mixed, too many air pockets are still trapped inside the meringue. Excess air expansion occurs during baking that can cause the macarons to crack. They will have a dull and porous appearance and usually contain no feet. The texture can be very chewy, dense, and dry, similar to meringue cookies, which is not what we intend to achieve. If the batter is over-mixed, almost all of the air pockets in the meringue will break down. In this case, not enough air expansion occurs during baking, the macarons will not rise properly, and they will produce no feet. When the batter is mixed properly, just the right amount of air pockets is broken down so that a "quasi-meringue" state is achieved in which the consistency of the meringue is between foam and liquid. In the quasi-meringue state, the right amount of air expansion during baking allows a glossy, thin shell to form on the macaron's exterior and a light, airy interior to develop and give shape to the feet. The mixing time depends on the stiffness of the meringue. If the meringue is soft, fewer strokes are required; if the meringue is stiff, more strokes are required. A simple consistency test is to lift up the batter with a spatula so that the batter cascades into the bowl in ribbons. The ribbons should disappear in approximately 10 to 18 seconds. A runnier batter produces flatter macarons with larger diameter; a thicker batter produces taller and smaller-diameter macarons with bigger feet. In any case, some experimenting may be required to achieve the optimal result.

4. Mix the powdered food coloring (if used) with the aged egg whites (**4, 5**). Add the colored egg whites to the reserved almond-sugar mixture (**6**). Mix all ingredients well with a spatula or bowl scraper until a thick, sticky paste has formed (**7**). Set aside.

5. For the Italian meringue, place the fresh egg whites in a 5-qt electric mixer bowl. Add the dried egg white powder (**8**). Attach the mixer bowl to the mixer fitted with the wire whisk attachment.

6. Cook the sugar and water in a saucepan over medium-high heat. Stir constantly until the sugar has dissolved. When the mixture comes to a boil, insert a candy thermometer and stop stirring (**9**). When the sugar syrup reaches 230°F/110°C, turn on the mixer and start to beat the egg whites at high speed.

7. When the sugar syrup reaches 244°F/118°C, slowly pour the syrup in a steady stream along the sides of the mixer bowl while the mixer is whisking (**10**). (Avoid pouring hot sugar syrup onto the rotating whisk; any splashed hot syrup can cause serious burns.) Continue to beat until stiff, glossy peaks form and the meringue has cooled to about 95°F/35°C (**11, 12**).

8. Mix the Italian meringue with the almond-sugar paste using a spatula or bowl scraper (**13, 14, 15**); mix until a soft, glossy batter forms. When lifted up with the spatula, the batter should flow back into the bowl in ribbons, and the ribbons should disappear in about 10 to 18 seconds (**16, 17, 18**).

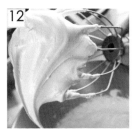

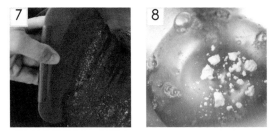

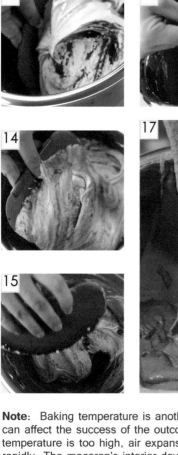

9. Preheat a conventional oven to 325°F/163°C (reduce the temperature to 300°F/149°C if a convection oven is used). Line a 13-in by 18-in/33-cm by 45.7-cm half-sheet pan with a half-sheet-sized silicone baking mat.

10. Fill a large pastry bag (18-in/45.7-cm) fitted with a ⅜-in/9.5-mm plain tip with the macaron batter **(19, 20)**. Pipe the mixture into 1-in/2.5-cm mounds, with 1-in/2.5-cm spacing, on the silicone baking mat **(21, 22)**. The mixture will spread out to about 1½-in/3.8-cm in diameter.

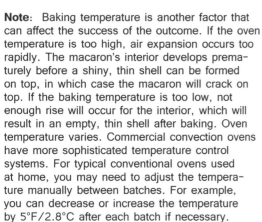

Note: Different people have different techniques for piping uniformly sized macarons. Some like to use a template with circles. Personally, I prefer a "counting" method that is easier and produces better results for me. For example, for 1½-in macarons, I count in my mind "one one thousand, two one thousand, three" while applying constant pressure to the piping bag fitted with a ⅜-in tip. This way I can maintain the flow of the batter at a relatively constant rate. The idea came to me from my piano-learning days. I used to accelerate uncontrollably when I was learning "Sonata Pathétique." My piano teacher, Ms. Van Derbur, suggested that I get a metronome or count in my head before I dislocated my shoulders. So, for those of you who had music or dance lessons, counting or humming a little rhythmic tune will make those macarons look like they were popped out by a machine.

Note: Baking temperature is another factor that can affect the success of the outcome. If the oven temperature is too high, air expansion occurs too rapidly. The macaron's interior develops prematurely before a shiny, thin shell can be formed on top, in which case the macaron will crack on top. If the baking temperature is too low, not enough rise will occur for the interior, which will result in an empty, thin shell after baking. Oven temperature varies. Commercial convection ovens have more sophisticated temperature control systems. For typical conventional ovens used at home, you may need to adjust the temperature manually between batches. For example, you can decrease or increase the temperature by 5°F/2.8°C after each batch if necessary.

11. Gently tap the baking pan against a hard surface to reduce air bubbles in the batter. Use a toothpick to pop any remaining air bubbles **(23)**. Bake the macaron shells for about 12 minutes on the upper-level rack in the oven **(24, 25)**. Remove the baking pan from the oven and place it on a cooling rack.

12. Let the macaron shells cool completely before removing them from the silicone mat **(26)**. Place them on a large clean surface with the smooth side up. Flip over half of the shells and pipe the filling onto the shells using a medium-sized (12-in/30.5-cm) pastry bag **(27, 28)**. Cover the piped filling with the remaining shells to make sandwiches **(29, 30)**.

13. Refrigerate the macarons overnight before serving. The macarons will stay fresh for about 3 to 4 days in the refrigerator or about 3 to 4 weeks stored in the freezer. Serve at room temperature.

Note: A half-sheet pan accommodates about 30 macaron shells. This recipe produces about 180 macaron shells that make about 90 filled macarons; bake them in batches if necessary. It is difficult to make Italian meringue with only one or two egg whites, especially with a stand mixer, and this is the reason for the portion size. You can make two or more types of macarons with different fillings.

BASIC CHOCOLATE GANACHE

In this recipe, we explain the technique of making the basic chocolate ganache filling. Chocolate ganache is an emulsion between chocolate and a liquid. The liquid ingredient can be cream, infused cream, fruit puree, or other types of flavoring agents. We present two methods for making the ganache. The first involves combining tempered chocolate with liquid cream under precisely controlled temperature conditions to produce a homogenous product. The second method is relatively less complicated; solid chocolate pieces are combined with hot liquid cream to achieve the desired result. Although the second method is simpler, we employ the first method throughout the book because it creates a ganache with a smoother mouth-feel, creamier flavor, and more refined texture.

Yield: Ganache filling for about 85 to 90 1½-in/3.8-cm macarons

INGREDIENTS

10 oz/284 g bittersweet chocolate, finely chopped

1 cup (8 fl oz/237 ml) heavy whipping cream

1 Tbsp (0.5 fl oz/15 ml) light corn syrup or glucose syrup

1 Tbsp (0.5 oz/14 g) unsalted butter, at room temperature

Liquid flavoring (optional)

Note: The quality of the chocolate is important. Use only the finest couverture baking chocolate for this recipe; some brands include Callebaut, Valrhona, and Scharffen Berger. In general, good-quality dark chocolate should contain at least 60% cocoa solids.

Method 1:

1. Add water to a small saucepan until about ⅓ full, and let simmer over low heat. Place a mixing bowl on top of the saucepan. Choose a mixing bowl that fits snugly on top of the saucepan; the bottom of the bowl must not touch the water. Place about ¾ of the chocolate pieces into this water bath, or double boiler **(1, 2)**.

2. Stir the chocolate with a spatula and monitor the temperature carefully **(3, 4)**. When the temperature reaches 120°F/49°C, take the mixing bowl off the saucepan. Do not heat the chocolate above 130°F/54°C and do not let any water drop into the chocolate.

3. Allow the melted chocolate to cool to 115°F/46°C. Add the remaining chocolate pieces and stir occasionally with a spatula **(5, 6)**. When the temperature drops to 90°F/32°C, the chocolate is ready for use.

4. Meanwhile, bring the cream and corn syrup to a boil in a medium-sized saucepan over medium-high heat **(7)**. Remove from heat and let cool to 105°F/40°C. Add the cream to the tempered chocolate and stir until the ganache is smooth **(8, 9)**.

5. Add the soft butter and liquid flavoring (if used) **(10, 11)**. Stir again to combine **(12, 13)**. Place the ganache in a container **(14)**. Cover the surface of the ganache directly with plastic wrap. Let the ganache solidify at room temperature for several hours or overnight. Use the ganache at room temperature **(15, 16, 17)**.

Note: For the ganache, tempered chocolate produces a finer texture and creamier mouth-feel. What is tempering? Solid chocolate couvertures at room temperature have perfectly arranged molecular structures between cocoa butter and cocoa mass, which are responsible for the glossy, firm appearance and snappy texture. This property is lost when the chocolate is heated because the fat crystals in cocoa butters become less stable. The chocolate must be tempered to reconstruct the original crystallized formation. Many chocolate-tempering techniques exist. In this recipe, we employ the "seeding" method, which is the simplest and most practical technique for small-batch home baking. In the seeding process, precise temperature control is crucial. I prefer to use a double boiler for tempering because the heat source is gentle and uniform. Using a microwave is another alternative although it can create random hot spots, which may result in uneven heating. If you use a microwave, stir the chocolate every 30 seconds to prevent burning.

Method 2:

1. Place the chocolate pieces in a medium-sized stainless steel mixing bowl. Set aside.

2. Bring the cream and corn syrup to a boil in a medium-sized saucepan over medium-high heat. Immediately pour the hot cream onto the chocolate pieces.

3. Allow the chocolate-cream mixture to sit undisturbed for about two minutes, and then stir with a spatula until the mixture is smooth. If there are any remaining solid chocolate pieces, place the ganache over a warm water bath to melt the chocolate. Do not heat the ganache above 94°F/34°C.

4. When the ganache has cooled to room temperature, stir in the soft butter and liquid flavoring (if used). Place the ganache in a container. Cover the surface of the ganache directly with plastic wrap. Let the ganache solidify at room temperature for several hours. Use the ganache at room temperature.

Note: It is best not to refrigerate the filling before piping it onto the macaron shells. The condensation created during refrigeration will make the macarons soggy and destroy the delicate interior. Warm or runny fillings will also make the macarons soggy.

SWISS MERINGUE BUTTERCREAM

Swiss meringue buttercream is light, creamy, and delicious. It is also very stable and relatively easy to make. We use Swiss meringue buttercream as the base for several filling recipes in this book.

Yield: Buttercream filling for about 85 to 90 1½-in/3.8-cm macarons

INGREDIENTS

4 oz/113 g fresh egg whites (about 4 egg whites), at room temperature

1 cup (7 oz/200 g) granulated sugar

1½ cups (12 oz/340 g) unsalted butter, at room temperature

Flavoring (optional)

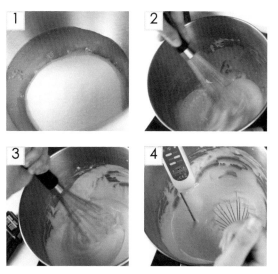

Note: To prevent the buttercream from curdling while incorporating the butter into the meringue, it is important to minimize the temperature difference between the meringue and the butter. Make sure both are at room temperature before combining them.

1. Combine egg whites and sugar in a 5-qt electric mixer bowl **(1)**. Place the bowl over a saucepan filled with simmering water over medium-low heat.

2. Beat the egg whites and sugar with a balloon whisk constantly until the mixture turns opaque, glossy, and warm to the touch (about 160°F/71°C) **(2, 3, 4)**.

3. Remove the mixer bowl from the water bath, and attach the bowl to the mixer fitted with the wire whisk attachment. Beat the mixture on high speed until stiff, glossy peaks form and the meringue has cooled to room temperature **(5)**.

4. Reduce the mixer speed to medium-low, and whisk in the soft butter in small increments **(6)**. Make sure each addition of butter is completely incorporated into the meringue before adding more butter. Scrape down the sides of the bowl with a spatula if necessary.

5. Once all of the butter is incorporated, adjust the mixer to medium-high speed. Continue to beat for a few more minutes or until the buttercream is light and fluffy **(7)**.

6. Add flavoring ingredients if used **(8)**. Whisk to combine **(9)**. Place the buttercream in a container. Cover the surface of the buttercream directly with plastic wrap. Use the buttercream at room temperature **(10)**.

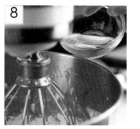

HAPPY HOUR SPECIAL

What makes happy hour even merrier? How about having your favorite cocktail in your favorite pastry? Indulge on macarons filled with margarita and cosmopolitan buttercreams; enjoy piña colada and mojito chocolate ganache. The afternoon cocktail hour will never be the same again.

MARGARITA

The main ingredient in a margarita cocktail is tequila. Tequila is a spirit distilled from the blue agave plant, which resembles a giant pineapple. I prefer to use good-quality tequila reposado, or "rested," in both the cocktail and this recipe. The reposado must be aged for at least two months. It has a smooth taste, but still maintains that bright, refreshing flavor.

Yield: 85 to 90 1½-in/3.8-cm macarons

Ingredients

Macaron Shells:

1 recipe Macaron Shells (page 12)

⅛ tsp (0.014 oz/0.4 g) yellow + ½₂ tsp (0.0035 oz/0.1 g) green powdered food coloring (optional)

Margarita Swiss Buttercream Filling:

1 recipe Swiss Meringue Buttercream (page 19)

Pinch of salt

1½ Tbsp (0.75 fl oz/22 ml) tequila reposado

1 Tbsp (0.5 fl oz/15 ml) fresh lime juice

2 tsp (0.33 fl oz/10 ml) Cointreau or Triple Sec

Zest of one lime

1. Follow the directions on page 12 to make the macaron shells. Add powdered food coloring if desired.

2. Follow the directions on page 19 to make the Swiss meringue buttercream. Whisk the salt, tequila, fresh lime juice, Cointreau or Triple Sec, and zest of one lime into the buttercream until well combined.

3. Pipe the buttercream filling onto half of the macaron shells using a medium-sized pastry bag. Cover the piped filling with the remaining shells to make sandwiches.

4. Refrigerate the macarons overnight before serving. Serve at room temperature.

PIÑA COLADA

You can make pineapple puree by processing fresh pineapple pieces in a food processor or blender. I prefer to use golden pineapples since they are sweet and tender. You can find cream of coconut in the liquor section of your local grocery store. Because cream of coconut is very sweet, we use a combination of white chocolate and cocoa butter to reduce the sweetness of the filling. Cocoa butter is one of the components extracted from the cocoa bean; the other component is called cocoa solids. Dark chocolate contains cocoa solids, cocoa butter, and sugar; milk chocolate contains additional milk product. White chocolate is made from cocoa butter, sugar, milk product, and vanilla flavoring, but contains no cocoa solids, and that is why white chocolate is sometimes not considered "true" chocolate.

Yield: 85 to 90 1½-in/3.8-cm macarons

INGREDIENTS

Macaron Shells:

1 recipe Macaron Shells (page 12)

⅛ tsp (0.014 oz/0.4 g) yellow powdered food coloring (optional)

Piña Colada Ganache Filling:

2 cups (18 oz/510 g) pineapple puree

1 Tbsp (0.5 fl oz/15 ml) light corn syrup or glucose syrup

10 oz (284 g) white chocolate, finely chopped

2 oz (57 g) cocoa butter, finely chopped

¼ cup (2 oz/57 g) cream of coconut (such as Coco Lopez), at room temperature

1 Tbsp (0.5 oz/14 g) unsalted butter, at room temperature

2 Tbsp (1 fl oz/30 ml) white rum

1. Follow the directions on page 12 to make the macaron shells. Add powdered food coloring if desired.

2. Follow the directions below to make the piña colada ganache filling.

3. Pipe the filling onto half of the macaron shells using a medium-sized pastry bag. Cover the piped filling with the remaining shells to make sandwiches.

4. Refrigerate the macarons overnight before serving. Serve at room temperature.

Piña Colada Ganache Filling:

1. Place the pineapple puree in a medium-sized saucepan over medium-high heat. When the puree comes to a boil, reduce the heat to medium. Stir constantly until the puree is reduced to ⅓ its original volume, approximately ⅔ cup (5.34 fl oz/158 ml). Add the corn syrup and stir to combine. Remove from heat and set aside.

2. Meanwhile, place about ¾ of the white chocolate pieces and the cocoa butter in a stainless steel mixing bowl. Place the bowl over a saucepan filled with simmering water over medium-low heat.

3. Stir the chocolate pieces constantly with a spatula until the temperature reaches 117°F/47°C. Remove the bowl from the water bath. When the chocolate temperature has dropped to 111°F/44°C, add the remaining chocolate pieces and stir. Let the chocolate cool to 86°F/30°C.

4. Add the warm pineapple puree (105°F/40°C) to the tempered chocolate, and stir until the ganache is smooth. Add the cream of coconut, soft butter, and white rum. Stir again to combine.

5. Place the ganache in a container. Cover the surface of the ganache directly with plastic wrap. Let the ganache solidify at room temperature for several hours or overnight. Use the ganache at room temperature.

COSMOPOLITAN

If you are a fan of the ever popular cosmo, then you will love these macarons. If you are not so fond of the cocktail, you will still love these macarons. They are delicate and tender, light and creamy, accented with a hint of cranberry, and sealed with a kiss of citrusy brilliance.

Yield: 85 to 90 1½-in/3.8-cm macarons

INGREDIENTS

Macaron Shells:

1 recipe Macaron Shells (page 12)

⅛ tsp (0.014 oz/0.4 g) red powdered food coloring (optional)

Cosmopolitan Swiss Buttercream Filling:

1 recipe Swiss Meringue Buttercream (page 19)

Pinch of salt

2 Tbsp (1 fl oz/30 ml) cranberry vodka

½ Tbsp (0.25 fl oz/7.5 ml) fresh lime juice

2 tsp (0.33 fl oz/10 ml) Cointreau or Triple Sec

1. Follow the directions on page 12 to make the macaron shells. Add powdered food coloring if desired.

2. Follow the directions on page 19 to make the Swiss meringue buttercream. Whisk the salt, cranberry vodka, lime juice, and Cointreau or Triple Sec into the buttercream until well combined.

3. Pipe the buttercream filling onto half of the macaron shells using a medium-sized pastry bag. Cover the piped filling with the remaining shells to make sandwiches.

4. Refrigerate the macarons overnight before serving. Serve at room temperature.

MOJITO

A refreshing concoction made of white rum, lime, and muddled mint leaves takes on a new identity when disguised with cacao and camouflaged between two lovely macaron shells. Some say that Hemingway used to frequent La Bodeguita del Medio for his mojito fix in Havana. I think he wouldn't mind his beloved cocktail's new look.

Yield: 85 to 90 1½-in/3.8-cm macarons

INGREDIENTS

Macaron Shells:

1 recipe Macaron Shells (page 12)

⅛ tsp (0.014 oz/0.4 g) green + ¹⁄₃₂ tsp (0.0035 oz/0.1 g) yellow powdered food coloring (optional)

Mojito Ganache Filling:

1 cup (8 fl oz/237 ml) heavy whipping cream

½ cup (0.5 oz/14 g) loosely packed fresh mint leaves

Zest of two medium-sized limes

4 oz (113 g) milk chocolate, finely chopped

6 oz (170 g) bittersweet chocolate, finely chopped

1 Tbsp (0.5 fl oz/15 ml) light corn syrup or glucose syrup

1 Tbsp (0.5 oz/14 g) unsalted butter, at room temperature

2 Tbsp (1 fl oz/30 ml) white rum

1. Follow the directions on page 12 to make the macaron shells. Add powdered food coloring if desired.

2. Follow the directions below to make the mojito ganache filling.

3. Pipe the filling onto half of the macaron shells using a medium-sized pastry bag. Cover the piped filling with the remaining shells to make sandwiches.

4. Refrigerate the macarons overnight before serving. Serve at room temperature.

Mojito Ganache Filling:

1. Place the cream, mint leaves, and lime zest in a medium-sized saucepan. Bring the mixture to a boil over medium-high heat. Remove from heat, cover the pan, and allow the mixture to infuse for 10 minutes.

2. Meanwhile, place about ¾ of the milk and dark chocolate pieces in a stainless steel mixing bowl. Place the bowl over a saucepan filled with simmering water over medium-low heat.

3. Stir the chocolate pieces constantly with a spatula until the temperature reaches 120°F/49°C. Remove the bowl from the water bath. When the chocolate temperature has dropped to 115°F/46°C, add the remaining chocolate pieces and stir. Let the chocolate cool to 90°F/32°C.

4. Meanwhile, bring the cream infusion back to a boil. Strain the mixture to remove the aromatics. Add the light corn syrup, and stir to combine. Set aside and let cool to 105°F/40°C.

5. Add the infused cream to the tempered chocolate, and stir until the ganache is smooth. Add the soft butter and rum. Stir again to combine.

6. Place the ganache in a container. Cover the surface of the ganache directly with plastic wrap. Let the ganache solidify at room temperature for several hours or overnight. Use the ganache at room temperature.

LOST IN PARADISE

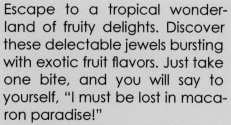

Escape to a tropical wonderland of fruity delights. Discover these delectable jewels bursting with exotic fruit flavors. Just take one bite, and you will say to yourself, "I must be lost in macaron paradise!"

Some people believe that one's life is defined by a few unforgettable events. If that's the case, then I have spent some of the most memorable moments of my life in the Amazon rainforest of Brazil. My adventure began in the city of Manaus, the capital of Amazonas. A five-hour bus ride and four-hour boat trip heading east took me into the heart of the river forest. I was on the Urubu River by nightfall; the warm and muggy tropical air was permeated with the pungent aroma of ripe fruits. I could vaguely see the silhouette of the tree line, both in the river and along the bank. It was the first time I had seen the Southern Hemisphere sky, and what an incredible sight! The sound of howler monkeys made me feel that I was among wild jungle creatures. Over the following days, I saw some of the world's most exotic fauna and flora, and that was the first time I tasted açaí palm berries. They have an appearance and taste similar to blueberries, but with a hint of green tea. Unlike most tropical fruits that have a pungent flavor, açaí is surprisingly mild, and yet addictive; it is absolutely divine when made into ice cream.

Yield: 85 to 90 1½-in/3.8-cm macarons

Ingredients

Macaron Shells:

1 recipe Macaron Shells (page 12)

⅛ tsp (0.014 oz/0.4 g) blue + ¹⁄₁₆ (0.007 oz/0.2 g) red powdered food coloring (optional)

Açaí Jam Filling:

1 cup + 2 Tbsp (8 oz/227 g) granulated sugar

1 tsp (0.14 oz/4 g) powdered pectin

1½ cups (13.5 oz/383 g) açaí puree

2 Tbsp (1 fl oz/30 ml) lemon juice

1. Follow the directions on page 12 to make the macaron shells. Add powdered food coloring if desired.

2. Follow the directions below to make the açaí jam filling.

3. Pipe the filling onto half of the macaron shells using a medium-sized pastry bag. Cover the piped filling with the remaining shells to make sandwiches.

4. Refrigerate the macarons overnight before serving. Serve at room temperature.

Açaí Jam Filling:

1. Combine the sugar and pectin in a stainless steel mixing bowl. Mix thoroughly and reserve.

2. In a medium-sized saucepan, combine the puree and lemon juice. Cook the mixture over medium-high heat until boiling.

3. Stir in the sugar-pectin mixture. Bring the mixture back to a boil and reduce the heat to medium-low. Stir constantly. Cook the mixture to 219°F/104°C, or a sugar density of 65° Brix, about 10 to 15 minutes.

4. Let cool slightly. Cover the surface of the jam directly with plastic wrap to prevent the sugar from crystallizing. Use the filling at room temperature.

BANANA RUM CARAMEL

The classic and timeless trio of banana, rum, and caramel is even more harmonious in a quintet with chocolate and macaron. I like to use dark rum in this recipe since its pronounced flavor will not fade away in the presence of chocolate and caramel.

Yield: 85 to 90 1½-in/3.8-cm macarons

Ingredients

Macaron Shells:

1 recipe Macaron Shells (page 12)

⅛ tsp (0.014 g/0.4 g) yellow powdered food coloring (optional)

Banana Rum Caramel Ganache Filling:

1 cup + 2 Tbsp (8 oz/227 g) granulated sugar

¼ cup (2 fl oz/59 ml) distilled water

½ cup (4 fl oz/118 ml) heavy whipping cream

2 ripe bananas, mashed into about ⅔ cup (6.3 oz/180 g) pulp

Pinch of salt

¼ cup (2 oz/57 g) unsalted butter, at room temperature

4 oz (113 g) bittersweet chocolate, finely chopped

6 oz (170 g) milk chocolate, finely chopped

2 Tbsp (1 fl oz/30 ml) dark rum

1. Follow the directions on page 12 to make the macaron shells. Add powdered food coloring if desired.

2. Follow the directions below to make the banana rum caramel ganache filling.

3. Pipe the filling onto half of the macaron shells using a medium-sized pastry bag. Cover the piped filling with the remaining shells to make sandwiches.

4. Refrigerate the macarons overnight before serving. Serve at room temperature.

Banana Rum Caramel Ganache Filling:

1. Place the sugar and water in a medium-sized saucepan over medium-high heat. Stir constantly until the sugar is dissolved. When the mixture comes to a boil, insert a candy thermometer and stop stirring. Continue to cook the sugar; brush down the sides of the pan with a pastry brush dipped in cold water to prevent sugar crystals from forming.

2. Meanwhile, place the cream in a small saucepan over medium heat and bring to a boil. Remove from heat and set aside.

3. When the sugar syrup temperature reaches 329°F/165°C, remove from heat. Carefully pour the hot cream into the syrup. Stir constantly. Return the pan to heat, and continue to cook for a minute or until the temperature returns to 230°F/110°C.

Add the banana pulp and salt; stir and cook the mixture until it boils.

4. Remove from heat. Place the banana caramel in a bowl. Let cool slightly. Stir in the butter and mix well. Cover the surface of the caramel directly with plastic wrap.

5. Meanwhile, place about ¾ of the dark and milk chocolate pieces in a stainless steel mixing bowl. Place the bowl over a saucepan filled with simmering water over medium-low heat.

6. Stir the chocolate pieces constantly with a spatula until the temperature reaches 120°F/49°C. Remove the bowl from the water bath. When the chocolate temperature has dropped to 115°F/46°C, add the remaining chocolate pieces and stir. Let the chocolate cool to 90°F/32°C.

7. Add the banana caramel and dark rum to the tempered chocolate. Stir to combine. If you don't like chunky banana pieces in the ganache, use a handheld immersion blender to process it for a few seconds until smooth.

8. Place the ganache in a container. Cover the surface of the ganache directly with plastic wrap. Let the ganache solidify at room temperature for several hours or overnight. Use the ganache at room temperature.

On one occasion, I was driving on Hana Highway on the island of Maui. A sudden downpour forced me to stop. After the storm passed, I wandered off along a hiking trail toward the sound of a cascading waterfall. I was captivated by the intoxicating aroma of ripe tropical fruit, and suddenly I was surrounded by a lush rainforest of guava and mango trees. A sea of fallen guavas was an irresistible sight. The fruit was sweet, tender, and juicy with pink flesh and soft seeds. It had the texture of soft pears and the fragrance of passion fruit. I always recall the amazing discovery I made in that tropical wonderland whenever I have these macarons.

Yield: 85 to 90 1½-in/3.8-cm macarons

INGREDIENTS

Macaron Shells:

1 recipe Macaron Shells (page 12)

¼ tsp (0.028 oz/0.8 g) red + ⅟₃₂ tsp (0.0035 oz/0.1 g) blue powdered food coloring (optional)

Guava Jam Filling:

1⅓ cups (9.4 oz/267 g) granulated sugar

¾ tsp (0.11 oz/3 g) powdered pectin

1½ cups (13.5 oz/383 g) pink guava puree

1. Follow the directions on page 12 to make the macaron shells. Add powdered food coloring if desired.

2. Follow the directions below to make the guava jam filling.

3. Pipe the filling onto half of the macaron shells using a medium-sized pastry bag. Cover the piped filling with the remaining shells to make sandwiches.

4. Refrigerate the macarons overnight before serving. Serve at room temperature.

Guava Jam Filling:

1. Combine the sugar and pectin in a stainless steel mixing bowl. Mix thoroughly and reserve.

2. In a medium-sized saucepan, cook the puree over medium-high heat until boiling.

3. Stir in the sugar-pectin mixture. Bring the mixture back to a boil and reduce the heat to medium-low. Stir constantly. Cook the mixture to 217°F/103°C, or a sugar density of 62° Brix, about 10 to 15 minutes.

4. Let cool slightly. Cover the surface of the jam directly with plastic wrap to prevent the sugar from crystallizing. Use the filling at room temperature.

MEYER LEMON

My parents have a few Meyer lemon trees in their home garden in Houston, Texas. During spring, these lemon trees bloom with beautiful, fragrant white blossoms, and each fall they are crowded with hundreds of lemons in lovely yellow clusters. Unlike the lemons from the market, these lemons are tree-ripened. The fruits are large, juicy, and blemish-free. The Meyer lemon skin is thin and smooth, with a delicate aroma. I like to make marmalade, lemon curd, and limoncello from these marvelous fruits. Of course, they are even more amazing sandwiched in between macarons.

Yield: 85 to 90 1½-in/3.8-cm macarons

INGREDIENTS

Macaron Shells:

1 recipe Macaron Shells (page 12)

⅛ tsp (0.014 oz/0.4 g) yellow powdered food coloring (optional)

Meyer Lemon Curd Swiss Buttercream Filling:

2 whole eggs (3.4 oz/96 g)

⅓ cup (2.35 oz/67 g) granulated sugar

Zest of 3 Meyer lemons

⅓ cup (2.67 fl oz/79 ml) Meyer lemon juice (the juice of about 3 lemons)

3 Tbsp (1.5 oz/43 g) unsalted butter, chilled

1 recipe Swiss Meringue Buttercream (page 19)

1. Follow the directions on page 12 to make the macaron shells. Add powdered food coloring if desired.

2. Follow the directions below to make the lemon curd Swiss buttercream filling.

3. Pipe the filling onto half of the macaron shells using a medium-sized pastry bag. Cover the piped filling with the remaining shells to make sandwiches.

4. Refrigerate the macarons overnight before serving. Serve at room temperature.

Meyer Lemon Curd Swiss Buttercream Filling:

1. In a medium-sized stainless steel mixing bowl, whisk the eggs and sugar with a balloon whisk until the mixture is light and fluffy.

2. Combine the lemon zest and lemon juice in a medium-sized saucepan. Bring the mixture to a boil over medium-high heat.

3. Pour the hot lemon juice and zest over the egg-sugar mixture while whisking vigorously. Pour the entire mixture back into the saucepan.

4. Whisking constantly, cook the mixture over low heat until it is thick and creamy.

5. Remove from heat. Let cool slightly. Whisk in the chilled butter until well combined. Set aside to cool.

6. Follow the directions on page 19 to make the Swiss meringue buttercream. Beat the room-temperature Meyer lemon curd into the buttercream until smooth.

COCONUT & LEMONGRASS

Coconut and lemongrass are not just for Thai curries anymore. This multi-talented duo has taken on a new role in the realm of pastry, dancing a tango of sweet delight while embraced by macarons.

Yield: 85 to 90 1½-in/3.8-cm macarons

INGREDIENTS

Macaron Shells:

1 recipe Macaron Shells (page 12)

⅛ tsp (0.014 oz/0.4 g) white powdered food coloring (optional)

Coconut & Lemongrass Ganache Filling:

⅔ cup (5.33 fl oz/158 ml) heavy whipping cream

¼ cup (1 oz/28 g) chopped lemongrass

10 oz (284 g) white chocolate, finely chopped

1 Tbsp (0.5 fl oz/15 ml) light corn syrup or glucose syrup

1 Tbsp (0.5 oz/14 g) unsalted butter, at room temperature

2 Tbsp (1 oz/28 g) cream of coconut (such as Coco Lopez), at room temperature

1. Follow the directions on page 12 to make the macaron shells. Add powdered food coloring if desired. To make a lemongrass design, before baking the macaron shells, fill a small pastry bag fitted with a small plain tip with green-color macaron batter. Pipe a small dot or a curved line on each macaron shell. Use a toothpick to make some swirls.

2. Follow the directions below to make the coconut & lemongrass ganache filling.

3. Pipe the filling onto half of the macaron shells using a medium-sized pastry bag. Cover the piped filling with the remaining shells to make sandwiches.

4. Refrigerate the macarons overnight before serving. Serve at room temperature.

Coconut & Lemongrass Ganache Filling:

1. Place the cream and chopped lemongrass in a medium-sized saucepan. Bring the mixture to a boil over medium-high heat. Remove from heat, cover the pan, and allow the mixture to infuse for 10 minutes.

2. Meanwhile, place about ¾ of the chocolate pieces in a stainless steel mixing bowl. Place the bowl over a saucepan filled with simmering water over medium-low heat.

3. Stir the chocolate pieces constantly with a spatula until the temperature reaches 117°F/47°C. Remove the bowl from the water bath. When the chocolate temperature has dropped to 111°F/44°C, add the remaining chocolate pieces and stir. Let the chocolate cool to 86°F/30°C.

4. Meanwhile, bring the cream infusion back to a boil. Strain the mixture to remove the aromatics. Add the light corn syrup, and stir to combine. Set aside and let cool to 105°F/40°C.

5. Add the infused cream to the tempered chocolate, and stir until the ganache is smooth. Add the soft butter and cream of coconut. Stir again to combine.

6. Place the ganache in a container. Cover the surface of the ganache directly with plastic wrap. Let the ganache solidify at room temperature for several hours or overnight. Use the ganache at room temperature.

NUTS ABOUT MACARONS!

It began one day when my mother asked me why I used almonds but not other types of nuts in my macarons. I thought I should explore other possibilities, just to be fair to the other nuts out there. I started with hazelnuts and pistachios, and then moved on to the more adventurous bitter almonds, peanuts, and cashews. How did the macarons come out? You be the judge. I think that after one taste you will go nuts for these nutty macarons.

Why put peanuts in a macaron? Why not! They taste great roasted, boiled, candied, fried, with salt, with sugar, with chocolate, and now in macarons. I have been living in Georgia and Virginia for almost twelve years, and peanuts are no stranger to me. In this recipe, the macarons are going peanuts all the way, both in the macaron shells and in the filling. If you are a fan of peanuts, then this will be a real home run for you.

Yield: 85 to 90 1½-in/3.8-cm macarons

Ingredients

Macaron Shells:

1 recipe Macaron Shells (page 12); replace the blanched whole almonds with:

2 cups + 2 Tbsp (10.58 oz/300 g) raw blanched peanuts

½ cup (2.5 oz/71 g) finely chopped toasted peanuts (optional)

Peanut Butter Swiss Buttercream Filling:

1½ cups (7.5 oz/213 g) finely chopped toasted peanuts

¼ cup (1.76 oz/50 g) granulated sugar

2 tsp (0.33 fl oz/10 ml) peanut oil

¼ tsp (0.05 oz/1.5 g) kosher salt

1 recipe Swiss Meringue Buttercream (page 19)

1. Follow the directions on page 12 to make the macaron shells. In step 3, replace the blanched whole almonds with raw blanched peanuts. Before baking the macaron shells, sprinkle chopped toasted peanuts on top if desired.

2. Follow the directions below to make the peanut butter Swiss buttercream filling.

3. Pipe the buttercream filling onto half of the macaron shells using a medium-sized pastry bag. Cover the piped filling with the remaining shells to make sandwiches.

4. Refrigerate the macarons overnight before serving. Serve at room temperature.

Peanut Butter Swiss Buttercream Filling:

1. To make the peanut butter, place the toasted peanuts, sugar, peanut oil, and salt in a food processor or blender. Process until a paste is formed. If the mixture is too thick to form a paste, add a few more drops of peanut oil. Reserve.

2. Follow the directions on page 19 to make the Swiss meringue buttercream. Mix ⅓ of the buttercream into the peanut butter until smooth and free of lumps. Blend in the remaining buttercream until well incorporated.

PISTACHIO

Many pistachio pastries use pistachio paste as the main ingredient. I love pistachio paste, but I think toasted pistachios give the macarons a nuttier and fresher taste. The toasted nuts are mixed into rich, creamy French buttercream that is sandwiched between almond-pistachio macaron shells. Be careful because they can be highly addictive!

Yield: 85 to 90 1½-in/3.8-cm macarons

INGREDIENTS

Macaron Shells:

1 recipe Macaron Shells (page 12); replace the blanched whole almonds with:

> 1 cup + 2 Tbsp (5.29 oz/150 g) raw shelled pistachios
>
> **+**
>
> 1 cup (5.29 oz/150 g) blanched whole almonds

Pistachio French Buttercream Filling:

1 whole egg (1.7 oz/48 g)

3 egg yolks (1.7 oz/48 g)

½ cup + 1 Tbsp (4 oz/113 g) granulated sugar

2 Tbsp (1 fl oz/30 ml) distilled water

¾ cup (6 oz/170 g) unsalted butter, at room temperature

¼ tsp (0.05 oz/1.5 g) kosher salt

1 cup (5 oz/142 g) finely chopped toasted pistachios

1. Follow the directions on page 12 to make the macaron shells. In step 3, replace the blanched whole almonds with a combination of raw shelled pistachios and blanched whole almonds.

2. Follow the directions below to make the pistachio French buttercream filling.

3. Pipe the buttercream filling onto half of the macaron shells using a medium-sized pastry bag. Cover the piped filling with the remaining shells to make sandwiches.

4. Refrigerate the macarons overnight before serving. Serve at room temperature.

Pistachio French Buttercream Filling:

1. Combine the whole egg and egg yolks in a 5-qt electric mixer bowl. Attach the mixer bowl to the mixer fitted with the wire whisk attachment.

2. Cook the sugar and water in a saucepan over medium-high heat. Stir constantly until the sugar has dissolved. When the mixture comes to a boil, insert a candy thermometer and stop stirring.

3. Meanwhile, turn on the mixer and start to beat the eggs at high speed until light and fluffy. When the sugar syrup reaches 241°F/116°C, slowly pour the syrup in a steady stream along the sides of the mixer bowl while the mixer is whisking. Continue to whisk until the mixture is cool to the touch.

4. Reduce the mixer speed to medium-low, and whisk in the soft butter in small increments. Make sure each addition of butter is completely incorporated before adding more butter.

5. Once all of the butter is incorporated, adjust the mixer to medium-high speed. Continue to beat for a few more minutes or until the buttercream is light and fluffy. Add the salt and toasted pistachios; mix until well combined.

HAZELNUT

Hazelnuts have to be my all-time favorite nut. I love to eat them roasted, baked in cookies and cakes, sprinkled on top of ice cream, coated with chocolate, and in macarons. My mother always buys hazelnuts in the shell after Christmas when they are on sale. The best tool for cracking these nuts is a hammer. My mother and I can crack ten pounds of hazelnuts in one morning. However, we do have to watch out for the chubby squirrels that lurk around when we are working outdoors!

Yield: 85 to 90 1½-in/3.8-cm macarons

INGREDIENTS

Macaron Shells:

1 recipe Macaron Shells (page 12); replace the blanched whole almonds with:

> 2 cups + 3 Tbsp (10.58 oz/300 g) whole natural hazelnuts

½ cup (2.5 oz/71 g) finely chopped toasted hazelnuts (optional)

Hazelnut French Buttercream Filling:

1 whole egg (1.7 oz/48 g)

3 egg yolks (1.7 oz/48 g)

½ cup + 1 Tbsp (4 oz/113 g) granulated sugar

2 Tbsp (1 fl oz/30 ml) distilled water

¾ cup (6 oz/170 g) unsalted butter, at room temperature

¼ tsp (0.05 oz/1.5 g) kosher salt

1 cup (5 oz/142 g) finely chopped toasted hazelnuts

1. Follow the directions on page 12 to make the macaron shells. In step 3, replace the blanched whole almonds with whole natural hazelnuts. Before baking the macaron shells, sprinkle chopped toasted hazelnuts on top if desired.

2. Follow the directions below to make the hazelnut French buttercream filling.

3. Pipe the buttercream filling onto half of the macaron shells using a medium-sized pastry bag. Cover the piped filling with the remaining shells to make sandwiches.

4. Refrigerate the macarons overnight before serving. Serve at room temperature.

Hazelnut French Buttercream Filling:

1. Combine the whole egg and egg yolks in a 5-qt electric mixer bowl. Attach the mixer bowl to the mixer fitted with the wire whisk attachment.

2. Cook the sugar and water in a saucepan over medium-high heat. Stir constantly until the sugar has dissolved. When the mixture comes to a boil, insert a candy thermometer and stop stirring.

3. Meanwhile, turn on the mixer and start to beat the eggs at high speed until light and fluffy. When the sugar syrup reaches 241°F/116°C, slowly pour the syrup in a steady stream along the sides of the mixer bowl while the mixer is whisking. Continue to whisk until the mixture is cool to the touch.

4. Reduce the mixer speed to medium-low, and whisk in the soft butter in small increments. Make sure each addition of butter is completely incorporated before adding more butter.

5. Once all of the butter is incorporated, adjust the mixer to medium-high speed. Continue to beat for a few more minutes or until the buttercream is light and fluffy. Add salt and toasted hazelnuts; mix until well combined.

BITTER ALMOND & AMARETTO

My mother loves the flavor of bitter almonds in pastries, cookies, and desserts. She suggested the idea of mixing some bitter almonds with the sweet almonds in the macarons. I decided to investigate the possibilities. The combination of the sweet almonds and the bitter almonds from apricot kernels gives these macarons an amaretti-like taste. The addition of amaretto liqueur, made from bitter almonds, further intensifies the almond flavor.

Yield: 85 to 90 1½-in/3.8-cm macarons

INGREDIENTS

Macaron Shells:

1 recipe Macaron Shells (page 12); replace the blanched whole almonds with:

> ¾ cup (3.53 oz/100 g) blanched bitter almond slices
>
> +
>
> 1⅓ cups (7.05 oz/200 g) blanched whole almonds

½ cup (2.4 oz/68 g) toasted bitter almond slices (optional)

Amaretto Ganache Filling:

1 recipe Basic Chocolate Ganache (page 16); replace the bittersweet chocolate with:

> 6 oz (170 g) bittersweet chocolate, finely chopped
>
> +
>
> 4 oz (113 g) milk chocolate, finely chopped

2 Tbsp (1 fl oz/30 ml) amaretto liqueur

1. Follow the directions on page 12 to make the macaron shells. In step 3, replace the blanched whole almonds with a combination of blanched bitter almond slices and blanched whole almonds. Before baking the macaron shells, sprinkle toasted bitter almond slices on top if desired.

2. Follow the directions on page 16 to make the basic chocolate ganache. In step 1, replace the bittersweet chocolate with a combination of bittersweet and milk chocolates. In step 5, mix in the amaretto liqueur until well combined.

3. Pipe the ganache filling onto half of the macaron shells using a medium-sized pastry bag. Cover the piped filling with the remaining shells to make sandwiches.

4. Refrigerate the macarons overnight before serving. Serve at room temperature.

CASHEW

It was in Brazil that I had freshly squeezed cashew apple juice for the first time. I was puzzled at the name since I did not know that the cashew nut is the kernel of the cashew fruit, which is attached to an accessory fruit that is shaped like an apple. Cashew apple juice is a pale yellowish green in color and has a refreshing, mild taste similar to a pear, with a hint of sweet green pepper.

Yield: 85 to 90 1½-in/3.8-cm macarons

INGREDIENTS

Macaron Shells:

1 recipe Macaron Shells (page 12); replace the blanched whole almonds with:

> 2 cups + 3 Tbsp (10.58 oz/300 g) raw cashews

Cashew Butter Swiss Buttercream Filling:

1½ cups (7.5 oz/213 g) finely chopped toasted cashew nuts

¼ cup (1.76 oz/50 g) granulated sugar

1½ Tbsp (0.75 fl oz/22.5 ml) peanut oil

3 Tbsp (1.5 fl oz/45 ml) honey

¼ tsp (0.05 oz/1.5 g) kosher salt

1 recipe Swiss Meringue Buttercream (page 19)

1. Follow the directions on page 12 to make macaron shells. In step 3, replace the blanched whole almonds with raw cashews.

2. Follow the directions below to make the cashew butter Swiss buttercream filling.

3. Pipe the buttercream filling onto half of the macaron shells using a medium-sized pastry bag. Cover the piped filling with the remaining shells to make sandwiches.

4. Refrigerate the macarons overnight before serving. Serve at room temperature.

Cashew Butter Swiss Buttercream Filling:

1. To make the cashew butter, place the toasted cashews, sugar, peanut oil, honey, and salt in a food processor or blender. Process until a paste is formed. If the mixture is too thick to form a paste, add a few more drops of peanut oil. Reserve.

2. Follow the directions on page 19 to make the Swiss meringue buttercream. Mix ⅓ of the buttercream into the cashew butter until smooth and free of lumps. Blend in the remaining buttercream until well incorporated.

BOURBON & PECAN

When I lived in Georgia, I used to go pecan picking in Lawrenceville, which is about thirty miles northeast of Atlanta. The pecans were extremely fresh and the price was definitely reasonable, fifty cents for a one-gallon bucket full of nuts. I did have to compete with the hungry squirrels that lived on the farm. I made pecan pies and pecan bars, and, of course, all with bourbon.

Yield: 85 to 90 1½-in/3.8-cm macarons

INGREDIENTS

Macaron Shells:

1 recipe Macaron Shells (page 12); replace the blanched whole almonds with:

> 1 cup (3.53 oz/100 g) pecan halves
>
> +
>
> 1⅓ cups (7.05 oz/200 g) blanched whole almonds

½ cup (2.5 oz/71 g) finely chopped toasted pecans (optional)

Bourbon & Pecan Swiss Buttercream Filling:

1 recipe Swiss Meringue Buttercream (page 19)

1½ cups (7.5 oz/213 g) finely chopped toasted pecans

¼ tsp (0.05 oz/1.5 g) kosher salt

2 Tbsp (1 fl oz/30 ml) bourbon whiskey

1. Follow the directions on page 12 to make the macaron shells. In step 3, replace the blanched whole almonds with a combination of pecan halves and blanched whole almonds. Before baking the macaron shells, sprinkle chopped toasted pecans on top if desired.

2. Follow the directions on page 19 to make the Swiss meringue buttercream. Mix in the toasted chopped pecans, salt, and bourbon whiskey until well combined.

3. Pipe the buttercream filling onto half of the macaron shells using a medium-sized pastry bag. Cover the piped filling with the remaining shells to make sandwiches.

4. Refrigerate the macarons overnight before serving. Serve at room temperature.

MORNING BAZAAR

Embark on a mouthwatering journey to experience delightful rose and sesame buttercreams, fig and saffron jam, and cardamom and ginger ganache. These exquisite little treats will take you to the bustling markets of Marrakesh, Istanbul, Goa, and Isfahan.

FIG & SAFFRON

Saffron, one of the most highly prized spices in the world, is not just for Spanish paella anymore. I first loved saffron in my rice dishes and winter vegetable stews. Then I discovered the allure of saffron in sweet cuisine. Paired with figs, saffron brings out the figginess in figs, but does not outshine them.

Yield: 85 to 90 1½-in/3.8-cm macarons

Ingredients

Macaron Shells:

1 recipe Macaron Shells (page 12)

⅛ tsp (0.014 oz/0.4 g) red + ⅛ tsp (0.014 oz/0.4 g) blue + ¹⁄₁₆ tsp (0.007 oz/0.2 g) yellow + ¹⁄₁₆ tsp (0.007 oz/0.2 g) black powdered food coloring (optional)

Fig & Saffron Jam Filling:

1 cup + 2 Tbsp (8 oz/227 g) granulated sugar

1 tsp (0.14 oz/4 g) powdered pectin

Pinch of saffron strands

1½ cups (13.5 oz/383 g) fig puree

2 Tbsp (1 fl oz/30 ml) lemon juice

1. Follow the directions on page 12 to make the macaron shells. Add powdered food coloring if desired.

2. Follow the directions below to make the fig & saffron jam filling.

3. Pipe the filling onto half of the macaron shells using a medium-sized pastry bag. Cover the piped filling with the remaining shells to make sandwiches.

4. Refrigerate the macarons overnight before serving. Serve at room temperature.

Fig & Saffron Jam Filling:

1. Combine the sugar and pectin in a stainless steel mixing bowl. Mix thoroughly and reserve.

2. Slightly crush the saffron strands with your hands. In a medium-sized saucepan, cook the puree, lemon juice, and saffron strands over medium-high heat until boiling.

3. Stir in the sugar-pectin mixture. Bring the mixture back to a boil and reduce the heat to medium-low. Stir constantly. Cook the mixture to 217°F/103°C, or a sugar density of 62° Brix, about 10 to 15 minutes.

4. Let cool slightly. Cover the surface of the jam directly with plastic wrap to prevent the sugar from crystallizing. Use the filling at room temperature.

CARDAMOM & GINGER

Cardamom is one of my favorite spices. Its versatility goes beyond the realm of savory cuisine. It is a wonderful ingredient in pastries and candies. Whenever recipes call for cinnamon, I add just a touch of cardamom with the cinnamon to give it an interesting twist. I think ginger is another perfect companion for cardamom. Together with chocolate, it makes a unique macaron.

Yield: 85 to 90 1½-in/3.8-cm macarons

Ingredients

Macaron Shells:

1 recipe Macaron Shells (page 12)

⅛ tsp (0.014 oz/0.4 g) white + ¹⁄₃₂ tsp (0.0035 oz/ 0.1 g) yellow + ¹⁄₆₄ tsp (0.0018 oz/0.05 g) black powdered food coloring (optional)

Cardamom powder for dusting (optional)

Cardamom & Ginger Ganache Filling:

1 cup (8 fl oz/237 ml) heavy whipping cream

12 whole cardamom pods, cut into halves

2 Tbsp (0.7 oz/20 g) coarsely chopped fresh ginger root

4 oz (113 g) bittersweet chocolate, finely chopped

6 oz (170 g) milk chocolate, finely chopped

1 Tbsp (0.5 fl oz/15 ml) light corn syrup or glucose syrup

1 Tbsp (0.5 oz/14 g) unsalted butter, at room temperature

1. Follow the directions on page 12 to make the macaron shells. Add powdered food coloring if desired. Before baking the macaron shells, dust cardamom powder on top if desired.

2. Follow the directions below to make the cardamom & ginger ganache filling.

3. Pipe the filling onto half of the macaron shells using a medium-sized pastry bag. Cover the piped filling with the remaining shells to make sandwiches.

4. Refrigerate the macarons overnight before serving. Serve at room temperature.

Cardamom & Ginger Ganache Filling:

1. Place the cream, cardamom pods, and chopped ginger in a medium-sized saucepan. Bring the mixture to a boil over medium-high heat. Remove from heat, cover the pan, and allow the mixture to infuse for 10 minutes.

2. Meanwhile, place about ¾ of the dark and milk chocolate pieces in a stainless steel mixing bowl. Place the bowl over a saucepan filled with simmering water over medium-low heat.

3. Stir the chocolate pieces constantly with a spatula until the temperature reaches 120°F/49°C. Remove the bowl from the water bath. When the chocolate temperature has dropped to 115°F/46°C, add the remaining chocolate pieces and stir. Let the chocolate cool to 90°F/32°C.

4. Meanwhile, bring the cream infusion back to a boil. Strain the mixture to remove the aromatics. Add the light corn syrup, and stir to combine. Set aside and let cool to 105°F/40°C.

5. Add the infused cream to the tempered chocolate, and stir until the ganache is smooth. Add the soft butter and stir again to combine.

6. Place the ganache in a container. Cover the surface of the ganache directly with plastic wrap. Let the ganache solidify at room temperature for several hours or overnight. Use the ganache at room temperature.

ROSE

Move over Turkish delight, step aside Gaz candy, rose has found a new home in macarons—velvety and luscious buttercream with a subtle hint of rose essence. Some say that beauty lies in simplicity and this couldn't be truer for a rose macaron.

Yield: 85 to 90 1½-in/3.8-cm macarons

INGREDIENTS

Macaron Shells:

1 recipe Macaron Shells (page 12)

⅜ tsp (0.042 oz/1.2 g) red + ¹⁄₁₆ tsp (0.007 oz/0.2 g) blue powdered food coloring (optional)

Rose Swiss Buttercream Filling:

1 recipe Swiss Meringue Buttercream (page 19)

3 Tbsp (1.5 fl oz/45 ml) rose water

1. Follow the directions on page 12 to make the macaron shells. Add powdered food coloring if desired.

2. Follow the directions on page 19 to make the Swiss meringue buttercream. Whisk the rose water into the buttercream until well combined.

3. Pipe the buttercream filling onto half of the macaron shells using a medium-sized pastry bag. Cover the piped filling with the remaining shells to make sandwiches.

4. Refrigerate the macarons overnight before serving. Serve at room temperature.

SESAME

"Open Sesame." Those magic words will lead you to newfound treasures in the tantalizing world of macarons. Homemade sesame paste is easy to prepare and packed with the essence of freshly toasted sesame seeds. Since white sesame seeds have relatively subtle flavor, the addition of toasted black sesame seeds produces a more robust sesame taste in the filling.

Yield: 85 to 90 1½-in/3.8-cm macarons

INGREDIENTS

Macaron Shells:

1 recipe Macaron Shells (page 12); replace the blanched whole almonds with:

> 1 cup + 3 Tbsp (5.29 oz/150 g) white sesame seeds
>
> +
>
> 1 cup (5.29 oz/150 g) blanched whole almonds

½ cup (2.4 oz/68 g) toasted mixed sesame seeds (optional)

Sesame Paste Swiss Buttercream Filling:

1 cup (4.5 oz/128 g) toasted white sesame seeds

½ cup (2.6 oz/75 g) toasted black sesame seeds

¼ cup (1.76 oz/50 g) granulated sugar

1½ Tbsp (0.75 fl oz/22.5 ml) cold pressed sesame oil or peanut oil

¼ tsp (0.05 oz/1.5 g) kosher salt

1 recipe Swiss Meringue Buttercream (page 19)

1. Follow the directions on page 12 to make the macaron shells. In step 3, replace the blanched whole almonds with a combination of white sesame seeds and blanched whole almonds. Before baking the macaron shells, sprinkle toasted mixed sesame seeds on top if desired.

2. Follow the directions below to make the sesame paste Swiss buttercream filling.

3. Pipe the buttercream filling onto half of the macaron shells using a medium-sized pastry bag. Cover the piped filling with the remaining shells to make sandwiches.

4. Refrigerate the macarons overnight before serving. Serve at room temperature.

Sesame Paste Swiss Buttercream Filling:

1. To make the sesame paste, place the toasted white and black sesame seeds, sugar, sesame oil, and salt in a food processor or blender. Process until a paste is formed. If the mixture is too thick to form a paste, add a few more drops of sesame oil. Reserve.

2. Follow the directions on page 19 to make the Swiss meringue buttercream. Mix ⅓ of the buttercream into the sesame paste until smooth and free of lumps. Blend in the remaining buttercream until well incorporated.

I LOVE COFFEE,
I LOVE TEA

"... I love the java jive and it loves me ..." Who can forget that jazzy little tune by The Ink Spots, especially if you are a coffee and tea lover? Now you can enjoy your morning coffee and afternoon tea with a few new companions. Indulge on macarons filled with espresso ganache, mocha caramel buttercream, and jasmine and Earl Grey ganache.

ESPRESSO

I love coffee. I could not have survived ten years of engineering school without coffee. I cannot imagine those twenty-four-hour study marathons before final exams, those last-minute crunches in the lab before project deadlines, and those countless research hours in the library without my cup of joe. Gradually, coffee became more than just a necessity for me, and I began to drink coffee purely for enjoyment. I started to notice the distinctive taste of different varieties of beans. During a trip to Costa Rica, I learned about the planting, harvesting, and processing of coffee beans. That was when I realized how little I knew about these amazing little cherries that I have depended on for so long.

Yield: 85 to 90 1½-in/3.8-cm macarons

INGREDIENTS

Macaron Shells:

1 recipe Macaron Shells (page 12)

³⁄₁₆ tsp (0.021 oz/0.6 g) yellow + ¹⁄₁₆ tsp (0.007 oz/0.2 g) black + ¹⁄₃₂ tsp (0.0035 oz/0.1 g) red powdered food coloring (optional)

Espresso powder for dusting (optional)

Espresso Ganache Filling:

½ cup (4 fl oz/118 ml) espresso (about 2 double shots) or strong coffee

¾ cup (6 fl oz/177 ml) heavy whipping cream

1 Tbsp (0.5 fl oz/15 ml) light corn syrup or glucose syrup

4 oz (113 g) milk chocolate, finely chopped

6 oz (170 g) bittersweet chocolate, finely chopped

1 Tbsp (0.5 oz/14 g) unsalted butter, at room temperature

1. Follow the directions on page 12 to make the macaron shells. Add powdered food coloring if desired. Before baking the macaron shells, dust espresso powder on top if desired.

2. Follow the directions below to make the espresso ganache filling.

3. Pipe the filling onto half of the macaron shells using a medium-sized pastry bag. Cover the piped filling with the remaining shells to make sandwiches.

4. Refrigerate the macarons overnight before serving. Serve at room temperature.

Espresso Ganache Filling:

1. Place the espresso coffee in a medium-sized saucepan over medium-high heat. When the coffee comes to a boil, reduce the heat to medium. Stir constantly until the coffee is reduced to half its original volume, approximately ¼ cup (2 fl oz/59 ml).

2. Stir in the cream and corn syrup. Bring the mixture back to a boil. Remove from heat and reserve.

3. Meanwhile, place about ¾ of the milk and dark chocolate pieces in a stainless steel mixing bowl. Place the bowl over a saucepan filled with simmering water over medium-low heat.

4. Stir the chocolate pieces constantly with a spatula until the temperature reaches 120°F/49°C. Remove the bowl from the water bath. When the chocolate temperature has dropped to 115°F/46°C, add the remaining chocolate pieces and stir. Let the chocolate cool to 90°F/32°C.

5. When the cream and coffee mixture has cooled to 105°F/40°C, add the mixture to the tempered chocolate, and stir until the ganache is smooth. Add the soft butter and stir again to combine.

6. Place the ganache in a container. Cover the surface of the ganache directly with plastic wrap. Let the ganache solidify at room temperature for several hours or overnight. Use the ganache at room temperature.

JASMINE TEA

I love the fragrance of jasmine flowers. My grandmother had jasmine plants in her home. The jasmine blossomed at night and she told me that the soothing aroma would chase nightmares away. I think it actually worked since I never had a bad dream when I slept in her home. Both my grandmother and my mother enjoy drinking jasmine tea. Originated in Fujian province of China, jasmine tea is made from green tea infused with jasmine flowers. To infuse the tea leaves with jasmine scent, the night-blooming jasmine flowers are mixed in and removed for a number of nights. Each intricate dragon phoenix jasmine pearl is hand rolled with green tea leaves to form its shape. In this recipe, the sweet and perfumed jasmine tea aroma complements the silky smooth chocolate ganache marvelously. I decorated these macarons with a lace of triple hearts to symbolize the love that my grandmother, my mother, and I share for our favorite tea, the love we have for life, and our love for one another.

Yield: 85 to 90 1½-in/3.8-cm macarons

INGREDIENTS

Macaron Shells:

1 recipe Macaron Shells (page 12)

⅛ tsp (0.014 oz/0.4 g) green + ¹⁄₆₄ tsp (0.0018 oz/0.05 g) black + ¹⁄₆₄ tsp (0.0018 oz/0.05 g) yellow powdered food coloring (optional)

Jasmine Tea Ganache Filling:

1 cup (8 fl oz/237 ml) heavy whipping cream

2 Tbsp (0.5 oz/14 g) dragon phoenix jasmine pearls or jasmine loose tea

10 oz (284 g) white chocolate, finely chopped

Pinch of salt

1 Tbsp (0.5 fl oz/15 ml) light corn syrup or glucose syrup

1 Tbsp (0.5 oz/14 g) unsalted butter, at room temperature

1. Follow the directions on page 12 to make the macaron shells. Add powdered food coloring if desired. To make the triple-heart design, before baking the macaron shells, fill a small pastry bag fitted with a small plain tip with natural-color macaron batter. Pipe three small dots along a circular contour on each macaron shell. Use a toothpick to make the hearts.

2. Follow the directions below to make the jasmine tea ganache filling.

3. Pipe the filling onto half of the macaron shells using a medium-sized pastry bag. Cover the piped filling with the remaining shells to make sandwiches.

4. Refrigerate the macarons overnight before serving. Serve at room temperature.

Jasmine Tea Ganache Filling:

1. Place the cream and jasmine tea in a medium-sized saucepan. Bring the mixture to a boil over medium-high heat. Remove from heat, cover the pan, and allow the mixture to infuse for 10 minutes.

2. Meanwhile, place about ¾ of the chocolate pieces in a stainless steel mixing bowl. Place the bowl over a saucepan filled with simmering water over medium-low heat.

3. Stir the chocolate pieces constantly with a spatula until the temperature reaches 117°F/47°C. Remove the bowl from the water bath. When the chocolate temperature has dropped to 111°F/44°C, add the remaining chocolate pieces and stir. Let the chocolate cool to 86°F/30°C.

4. Meanwhile, bring the cream infusion back to a boil. Strain the mixture to remove the tea leaves. Add the salt and light corn syrup, and stir to combine. Set aside and let cool to 105°F/40°C.

5. Add the infused cream to the tempered chocolate, and stir until the ganache is smooth. Add the soft butter and stir again to combine.

6. Place the ganache in a container. Cover the surface of the ganache directly with plastic wrap. Let the ganache solidify at room temperature for several hours or overnight. Use the ganache at room temperature.

MOCHA CARAMEL

My coffee obsession was elevated to new heights a few years ago when I started to roast my own beans. My secret blend includes one part Yemen, one part Costa Rica, and two parts Sumatra. I think the aroma of freshly roasted coffee beans is absolutely amazing, although my smoke alarm seems to disagree with me. Use good-quality Arabica beans such as mocha for this recipe. The complex, aromatic flavor of the Arabica beans is perfectly balanced with the sweet, silky caramel buttercream.

Yield: 85 to 90 1½-in/3.8-cm macarons

INGREDIENTS

Macaron Shells:

1 recipe Macaron Shells (page 12)

¼ tsp (0.028 oz/0.8 g) yellow + ⅓₂ tsp (0.0035 oz/0.1 g) black + ⅓₂ tsp (0.0035 oz/0.1 g) red powdered food coloring (optional)

Mocha Caramel Buttercream Filling:

1⅔ cups (11.75 oz/333 g) granulated sugar

6 Tbsp (3 fl oz/89 ml) distilled water

½ cup (4 fl oz/118 ml) espresso (about 2 double shots) or strong coffee, preferably brewed with Arabica coffee beans

Pinch of salt

1 cup (8 oz/227 g) unsalted butter, at room temperature

1. Follow the directions on page 12 to make the macaron shells. Add powdered food coloring if desired. To make the mocha swirl design, before baking the macaron shells, fill a small pastry bag fitted with a small plain tip with brown-color macaron batter. Pipe a small dot or a curve on each macaron shell. Use a toothpick to make some swirls.

2. Follow the directions below to make the mocha caramel buttercream filling.

3. Pipe the filling onto half of the macaron shells using a medium-sized pastry bag. Cover the piped filling with the remaining shells to make sandwiches.

4. Refrigerate the macarons overnight before serving. Serve at room temperature.

Mocha Caramel Buttercream Filling:

1. Place the sugar and water in a medium-sized saucepan over medium-high heat. Stir constantly until the sugar is dissolved. When the mixture comes to a boil, insert a candy thermometer and stop stirring. Continue to cook the sugar; brush down the sides of the pan with a pastry brush dipped in cold water to prevent sugar crystals from forming.

2. Meanwhile, place the coffee in a small saucepan over medium heat and bring to a boil. Remove from heat and set aside.

3. When the sugar syrup temperature reaches 329°F/165°C, remove from heat. Carefully pour the hot coffee into the syrup. Stir constantly. Return the pan to heat, and continue to cook for a minute or until the temperature returns to 230°F/110°C. Add salt and stir to combine.

4. Remove from heat. Place the mocha caramel in a bowl. Let cool slightly. Cover the surface of the mocha caramel directly with plastic wrap.

5. When the mocha caramel has cooled to room temperature, beat the soft butter with an electric mixer fitted with the wire whisk attachment until light and fluffy. Add the mocha caramel. Continue to beat until the mocha caramel is fully incorporated into the butter.

EARL GREY TEA

Named after Earl Charles Grey, British Prime Minister in the 1830s, Earl Grey tea is usually composed of a blend of Ceylon and Nilgiri teas and the bergamot citrus rind. The intense and full-bodied flavor of this tea blend goes perfectly with the smooth, creamy chocolate ganache.

Yield: 85 to 90 1½-in/3.8-cm macarons

INGREDIENTS

Macaron Shells:

1 recipe Macaron Shells (page 12)

⅛ tsp (0.014 oz/0.4 g) yellow + ¹⁄₃₂ tsp (0.0035 oz/0.1 g) black + ¹⁄₃₂ tsp (0.0035 oz/0.1 g) red powdered food coloring (optional)

Earl Grey Tea Ganache Filling:

1 cup (8 fl oz/237 ml) heavy whipping cream

2 Tbsp (0.5 oz/14 g) Blue Flower Earl Grey loose tea

4 oz (113 g) bittersweet chocolate, finely chopped

6 oz (170 g) milk chocolate, finely chopped

1 Tbsp (0.5 fl oz/15 ml) light corn syrup or glucose syrup

1 Tbsp (0.5 oz/14 g) unsalted butter, at room temperature

1. Follow the directions on page 12 to make the macaron shells. Add powdered food coloring if desired.

2. Follow the directions below to make the Earl Grey tea ganache filling.

3. Pipe the filling onto half of the macaron shells using a medium-sized pastry bag. Cover the piped filling with the remaining shells to make sandwiches.

4. Refrigerate the macarons overnight before serving. Serve at room temperature.

Earl Grey Tea Ganache Filling:

1. Place the cream and Earl Grey tea in a medium-sized saucepan. Bring the mixture to a boil over medium-high heat. Remove from heat, cover the pan, and allow the mixture to infuse for 10 minutes.

2. Meanwhile, place about ¾ of the dark and milk chocolate pieces in a stainless steel mixing bowl. Place the bowl over a saucepan filled with simmering water over medium-low heat.

3. Stir the chocolate pieces constantly with a spatula until the temperature reaches 120°F/49°C. Remove the bowl from the water bath. When the chocolate temperature has dropped to 115°F/46°C, add the remaining chocolate pieces and stir. Let the chocolate cool to 90°F/32°C.

4. Meanwhile, bring the cream infusion back to a boil. Strain the mixture to remove the tea leaves. Add the light corn syrup, and stir to combine. Set aside and let cool to 105°F/40°C.

5. Add the infused cream to the tempered chocolate, and stir until the ganache is smooth. Add the soft butter and stir again to combine.

6. Place the ganache in a container. Cover the surface of the ganache directly with plastic wrap. Let the ganache solidify at room temperature for several hours or overnight. Use the ganache at room temperature.

WOW, LOOK AT THOSE LITTLE HAMBURGERS!

One of my colleagues at NASA told me that my macarons look like little hamburgers. This inspired me to use ingredients that are traditionally associated with savory dishes. Our sweet-and-savory macaron adventure includes maple bacon buttercream, jalapeño pepper jam, spicy mango salsa, and green peas with wasabi.

MAPLE BACON

If you are going to try only one recipe from this book, then this is the one you ought to make. The combination of maple, bacon, and macaron is sweet, salty, smoky, and brought together by buttery, velvety French buttercream. It is the ultimate sweet-and-savory experience that you will become addicted to after just one bite.

Yield: 85 to 90 1½-in/3.8-cm macarons

INGREDIENTS

Macaron Shells:

1 recipe Macaron Shells (page 12)

⅛ tsp (0.014 oz/0.4 g) yellow + ¹⁄₆₄ tsp (0.0018 oz/0.05 g) red + ¹⁄₆₄ tsp (0.0018 oz/0.05 g) black powdered food coloring (optional)

Maple Bacon French Buttercream Filling:

2 whole eggs (3.4 oz/96 g)

6 egg yolks (3.4 oz/96 g)

1 cup (8 fl oz/237 ml) grade A medium amber maple syrup

1½ cups (12 oz/340 g) unsalted butter, at room temperature

9 strips of cooked bacon, finely chopped, about ¾ cup (2.4 oz/68 g)

1. Follow the directions on page 12 to make the macaron shells. Add powdered food coloring if desired.

2. Follow the directions below to make the maple bacon French buttercream filling.

3. Pipe the buttercream filling onto half of the macaron shells using a medium-sized pastry bag. Cover the piped filling with the remaining shells to make sandwiches.

4. Refrigerate the macarons overnight before serving. Serve at room temperature.

Maple Bacon French Buttercream Filling:

1. Combine the whole eggs and egg yolks in a 5-qt electric mixer bowl. Attach the mixer bowl to the mixer fitted with the wire whisk attachment.

2. Cook the maple syrup in a saucepan over medium-high heat. When the syrup comes to a boil, insert a candy thermometer.

3. Meanwhile, turn on the mixer and start to beat the eggs at high speed until light and fluffy. When the maple syrup reaches 241°F/116°C, slowly pour the syrup in a steady stream along the sides of the mixer bowl while the mixer is whisking. Continue to whisk until the mixture is cool to the touch.

4. Reduce the mixer speed to medium-low, and whisk in the soft butter in small increments. Make sure each addition of butter is completely incorporated before adding more butter.

5. Once all of the butter is incorporated, adjust the mixer to medium-high speed. Continue to beat for a few more minutes or until the buttercream is light and fluffy. Add bacon bits; mix until well combined.

JALAPEÑO PEPPER

These little chili peppers' resourcefulness is undeniable. They can be fried, stuffed, stewed, used in mixed drinks, and made into jelly and jam. The taste of jalapeño pepper jam is sweet, tangy, and refreshing, with just enough heat to make an impression. My mother first suggested that I put jalapeño pepper jam in macarons and what a fantastic idea!

Yield: 85 to 90 1½-in/3.8-cm macarons

INGREDIENTS

Macaron Shells:

1 recipe Macaron Shells (page 12)

¼ tsp (0.028 oz/0.8 g) green powdered food coloring (optional)

Jalapeño Pepper Jam Filling:

1½ cups (6 oz/170 g) seeded, stemmed, and chopped jalapeño peppers

1 cup (4 oz/113 g) seeded, stemmed, and chopped green bell peppers

½ cup (4 fl oz/118 ml) apple cider vinegar

1⅔ cups (11.75 oz/333 g) granulated sugar

1½ tsp (0.21 oz/6 g) powdered pectin

1. Follow the directions on page 12 to make the macaron shells. Add powdered food coloring if desired.

2. Follow the directions below to make the jalapeño pepper jam filling.

3. Pipe the filling onto half of the macaron shells using a medium-sized pastry bag. Cover the piped filling with the remaining shells to make sandwiches.

4. Refrigerate the macarons overnight before serving. Serve at room temperature.

Jalapeño Pepper Jam Filling:

1. In a food processor, combine the chopped jalapeño peppers, green bell peppers, and apple cider vinegar. Process the mixture into a puree.

2. Combine the sugar and pectin in a stainless steel mixing bowl. Mix thoroughly and reserve.

3. In a medium-sized saucepan, cook the pepper-vinegar puree over medium-high heat until boiling.

4. Stir in the sugar-pectin mixture. Bring the mixture back to a boil and reduce the heat to medium-low. Stir constantly. Cook the mixture to 219°F/104°C, or a sugar density of 65° Brix, about 10 to 15 minutes.

5. Let cool slightly. Cover the surface of the jam directly with plastic wrap to prevent the sugar from crystallizing. Use the filling at room temperature.

SPICY MANGO SALSA

Mango is another remarkably versatile tropical fruit that is splendid in both sweet and savory dishes. In this recipe, mango dances a salsa of deliciousness with a splash of lime juice, fresh cilantro leaves, and plenty of heat delivered by serrano peppers.

Yield: 85 to 90 1½-in/3.8-cm macarons

INGREDIENTS

Macaron Shells:

1 recipe Macaron Shells (page 12)

¼ tsp (0.028 oz/0.8 g) yellow + ⅛ tsp (0.014 oz/0.4 g) red powdered food coloring (optional)

Spicy Mango Salsa Jam Filling:

1½ cups (13.5 oz/383 g) mango puree

2 Tbsp (1 fl oz/30 ml) lime juice

½ cup (0.56 oz/16 g) cilantro leaves

2 medium-sized serrano peppers, seeded, stemmed, and chopped (about 2 Tbsp (1 oz/28 g))

1⅓ cups (9.4 oz/267 g) granulated sugar

¾ tsp (0.11 oz/3 g) powdered pectin

1. Follow the directions on page 12 to make the macaron shells. Add powdered food coloring if desired. To make the chili pepper design, before baking the macaron shells, fill a small pastry bag fitted with a small plain tip with green-color macaron batter. Pipe a curved line on each macaron shell. Use a toothpick to make the chili pepper shape.

2. Follow the directions below to make the spicy mango salsa jam filling.

3. Pipe the filling onto half of the macaron shells using a medium-sized pastry bag. Cover the piped filling with the remaining shells to make sandwiches.

4. Refrigerate the macarons overnight before serving. Serve at room temperature.

Spicy Mango Salsa Jam Filling:

1. In a food processor, combine the mango puree, lime juice, cilantro leaves, and chopped serrano peppers. Process the mixture into a puree.

2. Combine the sugar and pectin in a stainless steel mixing bowl. Mix thoroughly and reserve.

3. In a medium-sized saucepan, cook the mango salsa puree over medium-high heat until boiling.

4. Stir in the sugar-pectin mixture. Bring the mixture back to a boil and reduce the heat to medium-low. Stir constantly. Cook the mixture to 219°F/104°C, or a sugar density of 65° Brix, about 10 to 15 minutes.

5. Let cool slightly. Cover the surface of the jam directly with plastic wrap to prevent the sugar from crystallizing. Use the filling at room temperature.

GREEN PEA & WASABI

The idea came to me when I was munching on wasabi-roasted peas. What an ingenious combination. Who would have thought that peas and wasabi go together so well? These macarons are filled with sweet and refreshing green peas with a touch of fiery, pungent wasabi that are blended into tangy cream-cheese buttercream. It is nothing short of another savory-sweet masterpiece.

Yield: 85 to 90 1½-in/3.8-cm macarons

INGREDIENTS

Macaron Shells:

1 recipe Macaron Shells (page 12)

⅛ tsp (0.014 oz/0.4 g) green + ¹⁄₁₆ tsp (0.007 oz/0.2 g) yellow powdered food coloring (optional)

Green Pea & Wasabi Cream-Cheese Filling:

1 cup (9 oz/255 g) green pea puree

1 cup (7 oz/200 g) granulated sugar

2 cups (16 oz/454 g) cream cheese, at room temperature

1 cup (8 oz/227 g) unsalted butter, at room temperature

1 tsp (0.07 oz/2 g) wasabi powder

Pinch of salt

1. Follow the directions on page 12 to make the macaron shells. Add powdered food coloring if desired.

2. Follow the directions below to make the green pea & wasabi cream-cheese filling.

3. Pipe the filling onto half of the macaron shells using a medium-sized pastry bag. Cover the piped filling with the remaining shells to make sandwiches.

4. Refrigerate the macarons overnight before serving. Serve at room temperature.

Green Pea & Wasabi Cream-Cheese Filling:

1. Place the green pea puree and sugar in a medium-sized saucepan over medium-high heat. When the mixture comes to a boil, reduce the heat to medium. Stir constantly until the mixture is reduced to half its original volume, approximately 1 cup (8 fl oz/237 ml).

2. Let cool slightly. Cover the surface of the reduced green pea puree directly with plastic wrap to prevent the sugar from crystallizing. Let cool completely.

3. Combine the soft cream cheese and butter in a 5-qt electric mixer bowl fitted with the paddle attachment. Beat the mixture until it is well combined.

4. Add the reduced green pea puree, wasabi powder, and salt. Continue to beat for a few more minutes until the filling is light and fluffy.

Celebrate the most memorable days of the year with macarons! From timeless classics to innovative creations to spectacular showpieces, these little wonders are pleasing to both the eye and the palate.

HOLIDAYS ARE COMING!

NEW YEAR'S EVE

Celebrate the new beginning with these delightful little gems made with your favorite bubbly. Select a champagne that you actually enjoy drinking since the flavor of the wine intensifies after it is made into jelly. You can substitute the citric acid with one tablespoon of lemon juice if you don't mind adding a little bit of citrusy taste to the filling.

CHAMPAGNE

Yield: 85 to 90 1½-in/3.8-cm macarons

INGREDIENTS

Macaron Shells:

1 recipe Macaron Shells (page 12)

¹⁄₃₂ tsp (0.0035 oz/0.1 g) yellow + ¹⁄₃₂ tsp (0.0035 oz/0.1 g) white powdered food coloring (optional)

Champagne Jelly Filling:

1²⁄₃ cups (11.76 oz/333 g) granulated sugar

1½ tsp (0.21 oz/6 g) powdered pectin

½ tsp (0.07 oz/2 g) citric acid

1½ cups (12 fl oz/356 ml) brut champagne or sparkling wine

1. Follow the directions on page 12 to make the macaron shells. Add powdered food coloring if desired.

2. Follow the directions below to make the champagne jelly filling.

3. Pipe the filling onto half of the macaron shells using a medium-sized pastry bag. Cover the piped filling with the remaining shells to make sandwiches.

4. Refrigerate the macarons overnight before serving. Serve at room temperature.

Champagne Jelly Filling:

1. Combine the sugar, pectin, and citric acid in a stainless steel mixing bowl. Mix thoroughly and reserve.

2. In a medium-sized saucepan, cook the champagne or sparkling wine over medium-high heat until boiling.

3. Stir in the sugar mixture. Bring the mixture back to a boil and reduce the heat to medium-low. Stir constantly. Cook the mixture to 219°F/104°C, or a sugar density of 65° Brix, about 10 to 15 minutes.

4. Let cool slightly. Cover the surface of the jelly directly with plastic wrap to prevent the sugar from crystallizing. Use the filling at room temperature.

VALENTINE'S DAY

For Valentine's Day celebration, we make two types of mini macarons filled with raspberry jam and passion fruit ganache. We divide the original recipe for macaron shells into two equal portions used for these two different fillings, and then present them with a dazzling showpiece.

Yield: 100 raspberry and 100 passion fruit 1-in/2.5-cm mini macarons

INGREDIENTS

Macaron Shells:

1 recipe Macaron Shells (page 12)

⅛ tsp (0.014 oz/0.4 g) red powdered food coloring for raspberry macaron shells

³⁄₁₆ tsp (0.021 oz/0.6 g) yellow + ¹⁄₃₂ tsp (0.0035 oz/0.1 g) red powdered food coloring for passion fruit macaron shells

Raspberry Jam Filling:

¾ cup (5.3 oz/150 g) granulated sugar

⅜ tsp (0.053 oz/1.5 g) powdered pectin

¾ cup (6.75 oz/191 g) raspberry puree

Passion Fruit Ganache Filling:

⅔ cup (6 oz/170 g) passion fruit puree

½ Tbsp (0.25 fl oz/7.5 ml) light corn syrup or glucose syrup

6 oz (170 g) white chocolate, finely chopped

½ Tbsp (0.25 oz/7 g) unsalted butter, at room temperature

MACARON SHELLS

Follow the directions on page 12 to make the macaron shells, except:

1. In step 4, divide the aged egg whites into two equal portions. Add raspberry coloring to one portion, and mix half of the almond-sugar mixture with the raspberry-color egg whites into a paste. Repeat to make the passion fruit paste using the other half of the egg whites, passion fruit coloring, and almond-sugar mixture.

2. Similarly, in step 8, divide the Italian meringue into two equal portions and mix them into the two different-color pastes.

3. Place the two types of batter into two separate pastry bags and pipe the mini macaron shells into 0.7-in/1.8-cm mounds. To make the heart design for the passion fruit macarons, before baking the macaron shells, fill a small pastry bag fitted with a small plain tip with red-color macaron batter. Pipe a small dot on each macaron shell. Use a toothpick to make the heart.

4. Bake the mini macaron shells at 305°F/152°C for 10 to 11 minutes.

RASPBERRY

1. Combine the sugar and pectin in a stainless steel mixing bowl. Mix thoroughly and reserve.

2. In a medium-sized saucepan, cook the puree over medium-high heat until boiling.

3. Stir in the sugar-pectin mixture. Bring the mixture back to a boil and reduce the heat to medium-low. Stir constantly. Cook the mixture to 219°F/104°C, or a sugar density of 65° Brix, about 10 minutes.

4. Let cool slightly. Cover the surface of the jam directly with plastic wrap to prevent the sugar from crystallizing. Let cool completely.

5. Pipe the raspberry jam onto half of the raspberry macaron shells using a medium-sized pastry bag. Cover the piped filling with the remaining shells to make sandwiches.

PASSION FRUIT

1. Place the passion fruit puree in a medium-sized saucepan over medium-high heat. When the puree comes to a boil, reduce the heat to medium. Stir constantly until the puree is reduced to half its original volume, approximately ⅓ cup (2.67 fl oz/79 ml). Stir in the corn syrup and set aside.

2. Meanwhile, place about ¾ of the chocolate pieces in a stainless steel mixing bowl. Place the bowl over a saucepan filled with simmering water over medium-low heat.

3. Stir the chocolate pieces constantly with a spatula until the temperature reaches 117°F/47°C. Remove the bowl from the water bath. When the chocolate temperature has dropped to 111°F/44°C, add the remaining chocolate pieces and stir. Let the chocolate cool to 86°F/30°C.

4. When the reduced puree has cooled to 105°F/40°C, add it to the tempered chocolate, and stir until the ganache is smooth. Add the soft butter and stir again to combine.

5. Place the ganache in a container. Cover the surface of the ganache directly with plastic wrap. Let the ganache solidify at room temperature for several hours or overnight.

6. Pipe the passion fruit ganache onto half of the passion fruit macaron shells using a medium-sized pastry bag. Cover the piped filling with the remaining shells to make sandwiches.

SHOWPIECE ASSEMBLY

1. Cover three 5-in/12.7-cm Styrofoam cubes with red drawing paper using double-sided tape. Use glue and/or toothpicks to stack the cubes with a slight offset. For easy transport, glue the cubes to a round wood board covered with red drawing paper.

2. Using a sharp needle and a ruler as a guide, make a pattern of 4 x 4 marks that represent the centers of the macarons on each face of the cubes with approximately 1.2-in/3-cm spacing.

3. Insert toothpicks at the marked locations at an 80° to 90° angle with respect to the surface of interest, leaving about ¼-in/0.64-cm to ½-in/1.27-cm of the toothpicks outside. If the toothpicks are too long, cut them in half and insert the cut side into the Styrofoam.

4. Attach the macarons to the cubes and arrange them in alternating colors. Decorate the top with pulled sugar roses and ribbons if desired.

ST. PATRICK'S DAY

Forget about green beer; try macarons filled with Irish cream ganache and Guinness caramel buttercream for this year's St. Patrick's Day celebration. The addition of Irish whiskey gives the Irish cream chocolate ganache an extra boost, and who knew that Guinness goes so well with caramel buttercream? There is no doubt that this duo will become a part of your holiday repertoire.

IRISH CREAM

Yield: 85 to 90 1½-in/3.8-cm macarons

INGREDIENTS

Macaron Shells:

1 recipe Macaron Shells (page 12)

⅛ tsp (0.014 oz/0.4 g) green + ¹⁄₃₂ tsp (0.0035 oz/0.1 g) white powdered food coloring (optional)

Irish Cream Ganache Filling:

1 recipe Basic Chocolate Ganache (page 16); replace the bittersweet chocolate with:

> 2 oz (57 g) bittersweet chocolate, finely chopped
> +
> 8 oz (227 g) milk chocolate, finely chopped

1½ Tbsp (0.75 fl oz/23 ml) Irish cream liqueur

1 Tbsp (0.5 fl oz/15 ml) Irish whiskey

1. Follow the directions on page 12 to make the macaron shells. Add powdered food coloring if desired.

2. Follow the directions on page 16 to make the basic chocolate ganache. In step 1, replace the bittersweet chocolate with a combination of bittersweet and milk chocolates. In step 5, mix in the Irish cream liqueur and Irish whiskey until well combined.

3. Pipe the filling onto half of the macaron shells using a medium-sized pastry bag. Cover the piped filling with the remaining shells to make sandwiches.

4. Refrigerate the macarons overnight before serving. Serve at room temperature.

GUINNESS BEER CARAMEL

Yield: 85 to 90 11/2-in/3.8-cm macarons

INGREDIENTS

Macaron Shells:

1 recipe Macaron Shells (page 12)

¼ tsp (0.028 oz/0.8 g) black + ⅛ tsp (0.014 oz/0.4 g) yellow powdered food coloring (optional)

Guinness Beer Caramel Buttercream Filling:

1½ cups (12 fl oz/356 ml) Guinness draught

1⅔ cups (11.75 oz/333 g) granulated sugar

6 Tbsp (3 fl oz/89 ml) distilled water

Pinch of salt

1 cup (8 oz/227 g) unsalted butter, at room temperature

1. Follow the directions on page 12 to make the macaron shells. Add powdered food coloring if desired. To make the shamrock design, before baking the macaron shells, fill a small pastry bag fitted with a small plain tip with green-color macaron batter. Pipe three small dots on each macaron shell. Use a toothpick to make the shamrock design.

2. Follow the directions below to make the Guinness beer caramel buttercream filling.

3. Pipe the filling onto half of the macaron shells using a medium-sized pastry bag. Cover the piped filling with the remaining shells to make sandwiches.

4. Refrigerate the macarons overnight before serving. Serve at room temperature.

Guinness Beer Caramel Buttercream Filling:

1. Place the beer in a medium-sized saucepan over medium-high heat. When the beer comes to a boil, reduce the heat to medium. Stir constantly until the beer is reduced to ⅓ its original volume, approximately ½ cup (4 fl oz/118 ml). Remove from heat and set aside.

2. Place the sugar and water in a medium-sized saucepan over medium-high heat. Stir constantly until the sugar is dissolved. When the mixture comes to a boil, insert a candy thermometer and stop stirring. Continue to cook the sugar; brush down the sides of the pan with a pastry brush dipped in cold water to prevent sugar crystals from forming.

3. When the sugar syrup temperature reaches 329°F/165°C, remove from heat. Carefully pour the warm beer reduction into the syrup. Stir constantly. Return the pan to heat, and continue to cook for a minute or until the temperature returns to 230°F/110°C. Add salt and stir to combine.

4. Remove from heat. Place the caramel in a bowl. Let cool slightly. Cover the surface of the caramel directly with plastic wrap.

5. When the caramel has cooled to room temperature, beat the soft butter with an electric mixer fitted with the wire whisk attachment until light and fluffy. Add the Guinness caramel. Continue to beat until the caramel is fully incorporated into the butter.

FOURTH OF JULY

This Fourth of July, impress your friends and family with a gorgeous "Stars and Stripes" macaron showpiece. We use the familiar flavors of vanilla, blueberry, and strawberry in this recipe, but add some extra twists.

Yield: 100 Tahitian vanilla, 100 blueberry, and 100 strawberry balsamic 1-in/2.5-cm mini macarons

Ingredients

Tahitian Vanilla Macaron Shells:

2 oz/57 g aged egg whites (about 2 egg whites), at room temperature

1 cup (5.29 oz/150 g) blanched whole almonds or 1⅓ cups (5.29 oz/150 g) blanched almond flour

¾ cup (5.29 oz/150 g) granulated sugar

⅛ tsp (0.014 oz/0.4 g) white powdered food coloring

Half of the Italian meringue

Italian Meringue for Vanilla Macarons:

4 oz/113 g fresh egg whites (about 4 egg whites), at room temperature

½ tsp (0.035 oz/1 g) dried egg white powder

1½ cups (10.58 oz/300 g) granulated sugar

⅓ cup (2.67 fl oz/79 ml) distilled water

Tahitian Vanilla Italian Buttercream Filling:

Remaining half of the Italian meringue

TAHITIAN VANILLA

There are three major varieties of vanilla bean: Mexican, Madagascar, and Tahitian. Packed with bold and familiar vanilla flavor, Madagascar vanilla is the most commonly known species. Tahitian vanilla is more complex, refined, and fruity in taste and is by far my favorite vanilla.

1. Follow the directions on page 12 to make the macaron shells, except:

   a. Replace the original ingredient portion with the new portion listed for this recipe. (Only a half portion of the almond-sugar paste is needed in this recipe.) In step 4, add vanilla coloring to the aged egg whites.

   b. In step 8, mix only half of the Italian meringue into the almond-sugar paste. Reserve the other half of the meringue for the vanilla buttercream.

   c. Pipe the mini macaron shells into 0.7-in/1.8-cm mounds. Bake the mini macaron shells at 305°F/152°C for 10 to 11 minutes.

2. To make the vanilla buttercream filling, whisk the soft butter into the remaining half of the room-temperature Italian meringue using an electric mixer fitted with a wire whisk attachment. Whisk at medium-low speed and add the soft butter in small increments.

3. Once all of the butter is incorporated, adjust the mixer to medium-high speed.

Continue to beat for a few more minutes or until the buttercream is light and fluffy.

4. Split the vanilla bean in half lengthwise with a knife. Use the back of the knife to scrape off the vanilla seeds. Add the vanilla seeds to the buttercream. Combine well.

5. Pipe the filling onto half of the macaron shells using a medium-sized pastry bag. Cover the piped filling with the remaining shells to make sandwiches.

BLUEBERRY AND STRAWBERRY BALSAMIC MACARON SHELLS

Follow the directions on page 12 to make the macaron shells, except:

   1. In step 4, divide the aged egg whites into two equal portions. Add blueberry coloring to one portion, and mix half of the almond-sugar mixture with the blueberry-color egg whites into a paste. Repeat to make the strawberry paste using the other half of the egg whites, strawberry coloring, and almond-sugar mixture.

   2. Similarly, in step 8, divide the Italian meringue into two equal portions and mix them into the two different-color pastes.

   3. Place the two types of batter into two separate pastry bags and pipe the mini macaron shells at 0.7-in/1.8-cm diameter. Bake the mini macaron shells at 305°F/152°C for 10 to 11 minutes.

1 cup (8 oz/227 g) unsalted butter, at room temperature

1 Tahitian vanilla bean

Strawberry and Blueberry Macaron Shells:

1 recipe Macaron Shells (page 12)

¼ tsp (0.028 oz/0.8 g) blue + ¹⁄₆₄ tsp (0.0018 oz/0.05 g) black powdered food coloring for blueberry macaron shells

¼ tsp (0.028 oz/0.8 g) red + ¹⁄₆₄ tsp (0.0018 oz/0.05 g) blue + ¹⁄₆₄ tsp (0.0018 oz/0.05 g) black powdered food coloring for strawberry macaron shells

Blueberry Jam Filling:

½ cup + 1 Tbsp (4 oz/113 g) granulated sugar

½ tsp (0.07 oz/2 g) powdered pectin

¾ cup (6.75 oz/191 g) blueberry puree

Strawberry Balsamic Ganache Filling:

⅔ cup (6 oz/170 g) strawberry puree

½ Tbsp (0.25 fl oz/7.5 ml) light corn syrup or glucose syrup

5 oz (142 g) white chocolate, finely chopped

½ Tbsp (0.25 oz/7 g) unsalted butter, at room temperature

½ Tbsp (0.25 fl oz/7.5 ml) aged balsamic vinegar

BLUEBERRY

1. Combine the sugar and pectin in a stainless steel mixing bowl. Mix thoroughly and reserve.

2. In a medium-sized saucepan, cook the puree over medium-high heat until boiling. Stir in the sugar-pectin mixture. Bring the mixture back to a boil and reduce the heat to medium-low. Stir constantly. Cook the mixture to 219°F/104°C, or a sugar density of 65° Brix, about 10 minutes.

3. Let cool slightly. Cover the surface of the jam directly with plastic wrap to prevent the sugar from crystallizing. Let cool completely.

4. Pipe the blueberry jam onto half of the blueberry macaron shells using a medium-sized pastry bag. Cover the piped filling with the remaining shells to make sandwiches.

STRAWBERRY BALSAMIC

1. Place the strawberry puree in a medium-sized saucepan over medium-high heat. When the puree comes to a boil, reduce the heat to medium. Stir constantly until the puree is reduced to half its original volume, approximately ⅓ cup (2.67 fl oz/79 ml). Stir in the corn syrup and set aside.

2. Meanwhile, place about ¾ of the chocolate pieces in a stainless steel mixing bowl. Place the bowl over a saucepan filled with simmering water over medium-low heat.

3. Stir the chocolate pieces constantly with a spatula until the temperature reaches 117°F/47°C. Remove the bowl from the water bath. When the chocolate temperature has dropped to 111°F/44°C, add the remaining chocolate pieces and stir. Let the chocolate cool to 86°F/30°C.

4. When the reduced puree has cooled to 105°F/40°C, add it to the tempered chocolate, and stir until the ganache is smooth. Add the soft butter and aged balsamic vinegar. Stir again to combine.

5. Cover the surface of the ganache directly with plastic wrap. Let the ganache solidify at room temperature. Pipe the strawberry ganache onto half of the strawberry macaron shells. Cover the piped filling with the remaining shells to make sandwiches.

SHOWPIECE ASSEMBLY

1. Cover a 7-in/17.8-cm Styrofoam cube with white drawing paper using double-sided tape. For easy transport, glue the cube to a round wood board.

2. Using a sharp needle and a ruler as a guide, make a pattern of 7 x 7 marks that represent the centers of the macarons on each face of the cube with approximately 1-in/2.54-cm spacing.

3. Insert toothpicks at the marked locations at an 80° to 90° angle with respect to the surface of interest, leaving about ¼-in/0.64-cm to ½-in/1.27-cm of the toothpicks outside. If the toothpicks are too long, cut them in half and insert the cut side into the Styrofoam.

4. Attach the macarons to the cube and arrange them into the "Stars and Stripes." Decorate the top with pulled sugar ribbons if desired.

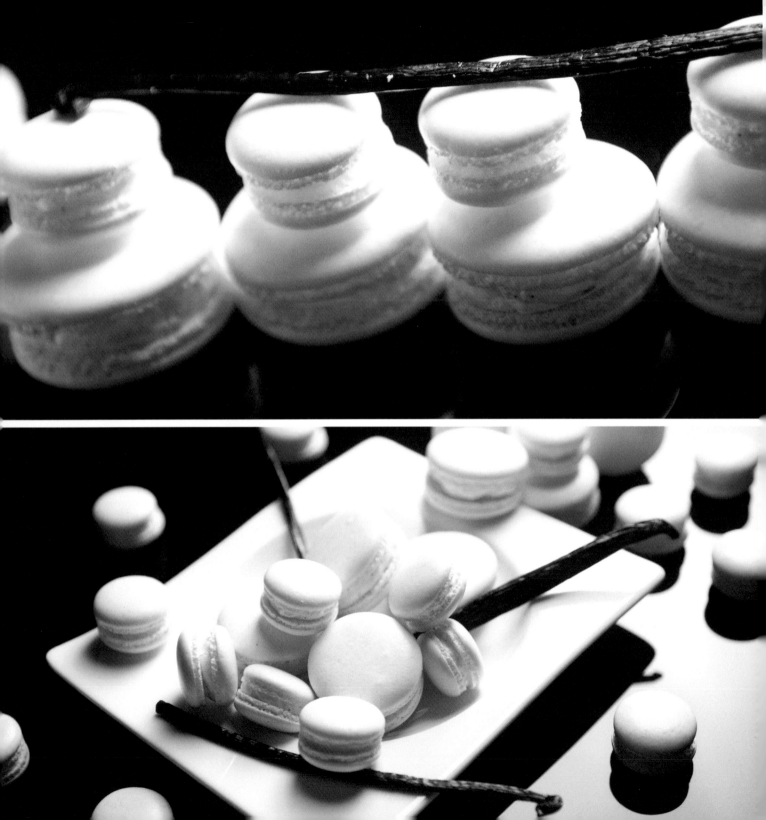

HALLOWEEN

Halloween without pumpkins and caramel apples is unthinkable. This year, create a sensation with these pumpkin-ginger and apple-caramel macarons. But beware, once the secret is out, those "trick-or-treaters" may never want to leave.

PUMPKIN & CANDIED GINGER

Yield: 85 to 90 1½-in/3.8-cm macarons

INGREDIENTS

Macaron Shells:

1 recipe Macaron Shells (page 12)

⅛ tsp (0.014 oz/0.4 g) yellow + ¹⁄₃₂ tsp (0.0035 oz/ 0.1 g) red powdered food coloring (optional)

Pumpkin & Candied Ginger Cream-Cheese Filling:

1 cup (9 oz/255 g) pumpkin puree

1 cup (7 oz/200 g) granulated sugar

2 cups (16 oz/454 g) cream cheese, at room temperature

1 cup (8 oz/227 g) unsalted butter, at room temperature

½ tsp (0.035 oz/1 g) cinnamon powder

¼ tsp (0.018 oz/0.5 g) nutmeg powder

¼ tsp (0.018 oz/0.5 g) allspice powder

¼ tsp (0.018 oz/0.5 g) ginger powder

⅔ cup (3 oz/85 g) finely chopped candied ginger

Pinch of salt

1. Follow the directions on page 12 to make the macaron shells. Add powdered food coloring if desired.

2. Follow the directions below to make the pumpkin & candied ginger cream-cheese filling.

3. Pipe the filling onto half of the macaron shells using a medium-sized pastry bag. Cover the piped filling with the remaining shells to make sandwiches.

4. Refrigerate the macarons overnight before serving. Serve at room temperature.

Pumpkin & Candied Ginger Cream-Cheese Filling:

1. Place the pumpkin puree and sugar in a medium-sized saucepan over medium-high heat. When the mixture comes to a boil, reduce the heat to medium. Stir constantly until the mixture is reduced to half its original volume, approximately 1 cup (8 fl oz/237 ml).

2. Let cool slightly. Cover the surface of the reduced pumpkin puree directly with plastic wrap to prevent the sugar from crystallizing. Let cool completely.

3. Combine the soft cream cheese and butter in a 5-qt electric mixer bowl fitted with the paddle attachment. Beat the mixture until it is well combined.

4. Add the reduced pumpkin puree, cinnamon, nutmeg, allspice, and ginger powders, candied ginger, and salt. Continue to beat for a few more minutes until the filling is light and fluffy.

APPLE CINNAMON CARAMEL

Yield: 85 to 90 1½-in/3.8-cm macarons

INGREDIENTS

Macaron Shells:

1 recipe Macaron Shells (page 12)

¼ tsp (0.028 oz/0.8 g) green + ⅟₁₆ tsp (0.007 oz/0.2 g) yellow powdered food coloring (optional)

Apple Cinnamon Caramel Buttercream Filling:

1 cup (9 oz/255 g) green apple puree

1⅔ cups (11.75 oz/333 g) granulated sugar

6 Tbsp (3 fl oz/89 ml) distilled water

Pinch of salt

1 cup (8 oz/227 g) unsalted butter, at room temperature

½ tsp (0.035 oz/1 g) cinnamon powder

1. Follow the directions on page 12 to make the macaron shells. Add powdered food coloring if desired. To make the apple design, before baking the macaron shells, fill a small pastry bag fitted with a small plain tip with natural-color macaron batter. Pipe a small dot or two dots on each macaron shell. Use a toothpick to make the apple design.

2. Follow the directions below to make the apple cinnamon caramel buttercream filling.

3. Pipe the filling onto half of the macaron shells using a medium-sized pastry bag. Cover the piped filling with the remaining shells to make sandwiches.

4. Refrigerate the macarons overnight before serving. Serve at room temperature.

Apple Cinnamon Caramel Buttercream Filling:

1. Place the apple puree in a medium-sized saucepan over medium-high heat. When the puree comes to a boil, reduce the heat to medium. Stir constantly until the puree is reduced to half its original volume, approximately ½ cup (4 fl oz/118 ml). Remove from heat and set aside.

2. Place the sugar and water in a medium-sized saucepan over medium-high heat. Stir constantly until the sugar is dissolved. When the mixture comes to a boil, insert a candy thermometer and stop stirring. Continue to cook the sugar; brush down the sides of the pan with a pastry brush dipped in cold water to prevent sugar crystals from forming.

3. When the sugar syrup temperature reaches 329°F/165°C, remove from heat. Carefully pour the warm apple puree into the syrup. Stir constantly. Return the pan to heat, and continue to cook for a minute or until the temperature returns to 230°F/110°C. Add salt and stir to combine.

4. Remove from heat. Place the caramel in a bowl. Let cool slightly. Cover the surface of the caramel directly with plastic wrap.

5. When the caramel has cooled to room temperature, beat the soft butter with an electric mixer fitted with the wire whisk attachment until light and fluffy. Add the apple caramel and cinnamon powder. Continue to beat until the caramel is fully incorporated into the butter.

THANKSGIVING

Cranberry, a Thanksgiving staple, is being reinvented this year. Let's start a new Thanksgiving tradition with these tender, sweet, and tart "superfruit" macarons.

CRANBERRY

Yield: 85 to 90 1½-in/3.8-cm macarons

INGREDIENTS

Macaron Shells:

1 recipe Macaron Shells (page 12)

⅜ tsp (0.042 oz/1.2 g) red + ¹⁄₃₂ tsp (0.0035 oz/0.1 g) black powdered food coloring (optional)

Cranberry Ganache Filling:

1⅓ cups (12 oz/340 g) cranberry puree

1 Tbsp (0.5 fl oz/15 ml) light corn syrup or glucose syrup

10 oz (284 g) white chocolate, finely chopped

1 Tbsp (0.5 oz/14 g) unsalted butter, at room temperature

1. Follow the directions on page 12 to make the macaron shells. Add powdered food coloring if desired.

2. Follow the directions below to make the cranberry ganache filling.

3. Pipe the filling onto half of the macaron shells using a medium-sized pastry bag. Cover the piped filling with the remaining shells to make sandwiches.

4. Refrigerate the macarons overnight before serving. Serve at room temperature.

Cranberry Ganache Filling:

1. Place the cranberry puree in a medium-sized saucepan over medium-high heat. When the puree comes to a boil, reduce the heat to medium. Stir constantly until the puree is reduced to half its original volume, approximately ⅔ cup (5.34 fl oz/158 ml). Stir in the corn syrup and set aside.

2. Meanwhile, place about ¾ of the chocolate pieces in a stainless steel mixing bowl. Place the bowl over a saucepan filled with simmering water over medium-low heat.

3. Stir the chocolate pieces constantly with a spatula until the temperature reaches 117°F/47°C. Remove the bowl from the water bath. When the chocolate temperature has dropped to 111°F/44°C, add the remaining chocolate pieces and stir. Let the chocolate cool to 86°F/30°C.

4. When the reduced puree has cooled to 105°F/40°C, add it to the tempered chocolate, and stir until the ganache is smooth. Add the soft butter and stir again to combine.

5. Place the ganache in a container. Cover the surface of the ganache directly with plastic wrap. Let the ganache solidify at room temperature for several hours or overnight. Use the ganache at room temperature.

CHRISTMAS

Create the most unforgettable Christmas memory with a spectacular macaron tower made with cherry and mint mini macarons. For the perfect Christmas present, a box of assorted macarons will definitely make a lasting impression.

Yield: 100 cherry and 100 mint 1-in/2.5-cm mini macarons

INGREDIENTS

Macaron Shells:

1 recipe Macaron Shells (page 12)

¼ tsp (0.028 oz/0.8 g) red + ⅟₃₂ tsp (0.0035 oz/0.1 g) black powdered food coloring for cherry macaron shells

¼ tsp (0.028 oz/0.8 g) green + ⅟₃₂ tsp (0.0035 oz/0.1 g) white powdered food coloring for mint macaron shells

Cherry Jam Filling:

¾ cup (5.3 oz/150 g) granulated sugar

⅜ tsp (0.053oz/1.5 g) powdered pectin

¾ cup (6.75 oz/191 g) cherry puree

Mint Ganache Filling:

½ cup (4 fl oz/118 ml) heavy whipping cream

⅓ cup (0.34 oz/9.3 g) loosely packed fresh mint leaves

2 oz (57 g) bittersweet chocolate, finely chopped

3 oz (85 g) milk chocolate, finely chopped

½ Tbsp (0.25 fl oz/7.5 ml) light corn syrup or glucose syrup

½ Tbsp (0.25 oz/7 g) unsalted butter, at room temperature

MACARON SHELLS

Follow the directions on page 12 to make the macaron shells, except:

1. In step 4, divide the aged egg whites into two equal portions. Add cherry coloring to one portion, and mix half of the almond-sugar mixture with the cherry-color egg whites into a paste. Repeat to make the mint paste using the other half of the egg whites, mint coloring, and almond-sugar mixture.

2. Similarly, in step 8, divide the Italian meringue into two equal portions and mix them into the two different-color pastes.

3. Place the two types of batter into two separate pastry bags and pipe the mini macaron shells into 0.7-in/1.8-cm mounds.

4. Bake the mini macaron shells at 305°F/152°C for 10 to 11 minutes.

CHERRY

1. Combine the sugar and pectin in a stainless steel mixing bowl. Mix thoroughly and reserve.

2. In a medium-sized saucepan, cook the puree over medium-high heat until boiling. Stir in the sugar-pectin mixture. Bring the mixture back to a boil and reduce the heat to medium-low. Stir constantly. Cook the mixture to 219°F/104°C, or a sugar density of 65° Brix, about 10 minutes.

3. Let cool slightly. Cover the surface of the jam directly with plastic wrap to prevent the sugar from crystallizing. Let cool completely.

4. Pipe the cherry jam onto half of the cherry macaron shells using a medium-sized pastry bag. Cover the piped filling with the remaining shells to make sandwiches.

MINT

1. Place the cream and mint leaves in a medium-sized saucepan. Bring the mixture to a boil over medium-high heat. Remove from heat, cover the pan, and allow the mixture to infuse for 10 minutes.

2. Meanwhile, place about ¾ of the dark and milk chocolate pieces in a stainless steel mixing bowl. Place the bowl over a saucepan filled with simmering water over medium-low heat.

3. Stir the chocolate pieces constantly with a spatula until the temperature reaches 120°F/49°C. Remove the bowl from the water bath. When the chocolate

temperature has dropped to 115°F/46°C, add the remaining chocolate pieces and stir. Let the chocolate cool to 90°F/32°C.

4. Meanwhile, bring the cream infusion back to a boil. Strain the mixture to remove the mint leaves. Add the light corn syrup, and stir to combine. Set aside and let cool to 105°F/40°C.

5. Add the infused cream to the tempered chocolate, and stir until the ganache is smooth. Add the soft butter and stir again to combine.

6. Cover the surface of the ganache directly with plastic wrap. Let the ganache solidify at room temperature. Pipe the mint ganache onto half of the mint macaron shells using a medium-sized pastry bag. Cover the piped filling with the remaining shells to make sandwiches.

SHOWPIECE ASSEMBLY

1. Cover a Styrofoam cone (18-in/45.7-cm height, 5-in/12.7-cm diameter) with green drawing paper using double-sided tape. For easy transport, glue the cone to a round wood board covered with red drawing paper.

2. Use a sharp needle to mark the cone at the locations that represent the centers of the macarons with approximately 1-in/2.54-cm spacing.

3. Insert toothpicks at the marked locations at a 90° angle with respect to the surface of interest, leaving about ¼-in/0.64-cm to ½-in/1.27-cm of the toothpicks outside. If the toothpicks are too long, cut them in half and insert the cut side into the Styrofoam. Attach the macarons to the cone and arrange them in alternating colors.

LIST OF RESOURCES

I think the best method for locating hard-to-find ingredients and baking tools is to conduct an internet search. For your reference, I have included a list of the stores where I shopped for the ingredients and tools used in this book.

For Pastry Equipment and Tools:

Amazon.com (www.amazon.com)
Chef Rubber (www.chefrubber.com)
JB Prince (www.jbprince.com)
Kerekes (www.bakedeco.com)
King Arthur Flour (www.kingarthurflour.com)
Pastry Chef Central (www.pastrychef.com)
Sur la Table (www.surlatable.com)
Williams-Sonoma (www.williams-sonoma.com)

For Pastry Ingredients:

Adagio Teas (www.adagio.com): loose tea leaves
Amazon.com (www.amazon.com): general pastry ingredients
American Almond Products Company (www.americanalmond.com): wholes nuts and nut flours
Arizona Vanilla Company (www.arizonavanilla.com): vanilla beans
Chef Rubber (www.chefrubber.com): general pastry ingredients
The Chefs' Warehouse (www.chefswarehouse.com): general pastry ingredients
Honeyville Food Products (www.honeyvillegrain.com): almond flours, dried egg whites
King Arthur Flour (www.kingarthurflour.com): general pastry ingredients
L'Epicerie (www.lepicerie.com): fruit purees
La Tienda (www.tienda.com): Spanish saffron
Marky's (www.markys.com): fruit purees
Pastry Chef Central (www.pastrychef.com): general pastry ingredients
Sambazon (www.sambazon.com): açaí puree
Teavana (www.teavana.com): loose tea leaves
World Wide Chocolate (www.worldwidechocolate.com): chocolates

CPSIA information can be obtained
at www.ICGtesting.com
Printed in the USA
LVIC06n1739150913
352531LV00002B